Carpe NOW

Carpe NOW

10 Habits to Master the Authentic You, Eliminate Excuses, & Create the Blueprint for Your Best Life

JAKE BARRENA

Carpe NOW

ISBN: 979-8-89109-553-3 - paperback
ISBN: 979-8-89109-555-7 - hardcover
ISBN: 979-8-89109-554-0 - ebook

Published by Barrena Corporation

For bulk sales and signed copies, contact the author by email.
Office@BarrenaCorporation.com
For interviews, contact me on my website: JakeBarrena.com

Cover design: Jomel Pepito
Editor: Margaret A. Harrell, https://margaretharrell.com

This book is dedicated to my legacy, which means everything to me. My legacy is not built on possessions but in people I love and adore.

My legacy is first to my children, Tenley Grace and Kingston James Barrena. You are my heart. Daddy loves you.

Next, my beautiful bride, Ashlee Britt Barrena. You are my missing rib and the keeper of my heart.

Mom and Dad, I am incredibly grateful for the both of you.

To my brothers, Jeffrey and Dylan, I am proud to have brothers that I consider close friends.

To all my other family and friends who are my chosen family, I love you all! I am a blessed man to have you.

To the people I have yet to meet, this book is also dedicated to you. Looking forward to our future connection.

CONTENTS

Be Present

Time to discover the authentic you

> One can have no smaller or greater
> mastery than mastery of oneself.
>
> —Leonardo da Vinci

Being fully transparent with yourself is key in your journey of discovery. Likewise, *being transparent with you* is of the utmost importance to me, one of the greatest values I can provide.

Let's begin by getting into the right state of mind for self-transformation. No one can expect to discover their authentic self unless they begin in the right state of mind. It's going to require some work and effort on your part. I am here with you, to guide you down a path of personal understanding and wisdom. To start this exciting journey, you will need to be in a quiet place. This quiet place looks different for each person.

Be utterly in the current moment. Do not allow life's circumstances or worries to intrude, to bog you down. Choose now to commit to this process. Discovering your authentic self is exactly that: a process that is going to take time and real effort. I am not talking about what other people tell you you are. We all have people in our lives who tell us who we are or who they believe we are. These people are all around us. They tell us how to think, what to say, whom to believe. Whether we are aware of it or not, we are all, *including me*, influenced by other people. All the time.

There is no person who has been alive, is alive, or will be alive that will not be influenced by others. This is a process of chiseling away at the preconceived ideas of who you believe you are. We are led by our beliefs, values, and circumstances. We either confidently believe we know who we are, or we question ourselves. We doubt our current circumstances and want more out of life. We want more out of ourselves. *Would it not be beautiful to know exactly who you are? Would there not be a sense of satisfaction knowing why you exist and your purpose in life?*

When you understand your personal mission in life, it's a game changer. I mean, who really knows their mission? Rare is that person. And if someone does know, what's that person like? Well, let me tell you. *That person would be on fire for life.* Have a passion that is unquenchable. A thirst that could not dry up. A drive that would relentlessly pursue a successful life. That person, in other words, would be truly unstoppable.

Do you want that to be you?

Why were you born in the first place? What in the world are any of us doing, alive in this era? Why have I been placed into the set of circumstances I currently live in? Being alive, you have, whether you realize it or not, countless choices ahead of you. Many thoughts that have not been previously thought. Decisions to be made and outcomes to be experienced. The unknown is in front of you. So many possible conclusions to reach and choices that will affect your life forever. *Are you ready for all life has to offer? How does that make you feel?*

Life is scary and daunting at times. Even if you live reclusively, you influence other people. Like it or not, you are an influencer.

With everything you have yet to face, are you ready for it? Do you know who you are? And if you believe you do know, I am sure there is still something in this book for you to learn and apply.

But, if you want more out of life—if you want to max out your life and are ready to discover your most authentic, absolute best version of yourself—then come along with me into this book. It is absolutely for you. *I have spent decades discovering and uncovering exactly who I am:* countless hours of self-reflection, reading, writing, developing, studying others, studying myself, finally achieving that no-longer-elusive goal. I am so excited about sharing what I have learned in my journey. I know what it takes to discover your authentic self. I cannot wait to be a part of your transformation.

Do not take the word "transformation" lightly. You've heard it said, "people do not change." I disagree. Change is at the crux of life. The first rule of change: you must believe you can change. You have the power within yourself. If you are ready to transform your life or maybe get a little tune-up or a course correction, don't wait. Transformations begin with those who lay it all on the line. Are you ready to lay yourself on the line? To expose all of yourself? *You must first expose who you are to yourself.* Then you can expose who you are to the world. That is when you become a world changer. One who is living life to the fullest. Holding absolutely nothing back from self or others.

Close your eyes, take a deep breath, quiet your mind, and let us spend a few moments taking an imaginary trip. Doing everything I just told you, begin this imaginary trip standing all alone in the middle of a desert, stripped down to nothing. By nothing I mean absolutely nothing: you do not own possessions, you belong to no one, no one knows you, you do not have a family name, you do not have status, your accomplishments have been forgotten, your failures have been forgiven, you have no food in your belly, and you literally do not have any clothes on your body. You are naked, by yourself; possess nothing to your name. Everything stripped away.

Now, having nothing, what is your first thought? Who do you say you are? What thoughts run through your mind? What fears? Can you see any positives?

When you take this imaginary trip, do you sense a complete honesty and transparency about who you are? Do you see yourself all alone, with a blank canvas to begin your journey? Are you ready to be vulnerable with who you are? This transparency is the beginning of your growth. If you cannot be honest with yourself, then you should not expect to discover anything about yourself. In order for this process to work, you must be brutally honest with how you see yourself. Strip away everything you possess and any picture of who you are. Does your life still have value? These are the answers you will discover about yourself. If you feel lost, broken, abandoned—that no one understands your pain—you need this book.

Many people are placing Band-Aids on wounds that are not surface level. They have deeper issues. Fundamentally, these issues are of the heart, mind, and soul. Not recognizing them is lying to yourself. If you are willing to move past all the layers of lies—beyond the surface—an abundantly beautiful life is yours to discover. A life full of joy and contentment—surrounded by happiness and peace. This newfound life will be genuine and true to who you authentically were created to be. Your authentic version is your best version. It is you living your best life. Not just existing but thriving each day to take in all that life has to offer.

In the quietness of my mind when I take this imaginary trip, I sense a weakness. In that weakness I am perplexed. Initially I do not fully understand it, but after some digging into my thoughts, I realize it stems from an inadequacy birthed from a place of wanting to seek my earthly father's approval. Wanting to be recognized and acknowledged by him. You see, growing up, I always wanted to be close to my dad, to have a relationship with him. I wanted him to notice me. I wanted him to *see me as the only person in the room.*

Unfortunately, that was not the case. You will read more about this later in the book.

Since then, I have laid those feelings to rest. I had to put in the work to understand why I had those feelings. I realized I needed to process those feelings and declared to myself a course correction for my life that would start with my children. My father and I now have a good relationship, which I am grateful for. But when I was growing up, my mind went to that place where I was seeking the approval of others because I never got that approval from my dad.

My heart in sharing this with you is exposing my vulnerability. Being vulnerable allows me to be transparent with where I have been and who I am. It exposes my darkest secrets. Exposes the things I do not want people to know about me. It forces me to be candid with others. These are the sort of answers that you must dig out of yourself in this process of discovering the authentic you.

You must leave your pride on the table and check your ego at the door as exposing your weaknesses leads you down the path of true transformation. If you want to elevate yourself to the level of knowing exactly who you are, you are going to have to bare all of you to the light. By bringing those struggles and weaknesses to light, you take away their power. *By giving up control, you start to gain control of the greatest version of yourself.*

No one is going to be able to assist you in discovering yourself. Yes, people can guide you down a path that is the right direction, but it is you who will have to face the challenges that lie ahead— not easy challenges. They will not leave you feeling warm and fuzzy inside. You will have to dig up past traumas and pains to realize your best version. If you can believe and trust the process in this book, a new self that has no limiting beliefs holding you back from taking your life to the next level is within your reach. Hold on tight, fasten your seatbelts, and get ready for the ride of your life. You will learn that:

- in order to be strong, you must first be weak.
- if you run from that weakness, then you are running from the very thing that will give you superhero-like strength. Take the hard road, discover your most authentic self by pursuing the very thing that causes you pain and anguish.
- it is time to put the spotlight on you. You are the one in the hot seat.

If you do not feel worthy of this abundant life, then this book is for you. If you feel that this life has no real value for you, then this book is for you. Do you struggle with the big questions in life—like, "Why am I here? What is my purpose? What am I to do with my life? What direction should I go in? Who am I? Really, who am I? Why have I been placed on this Earth?"—then this book is for you.

If you feel lost, alone, broken, abandoned, bedraggled, beaten up, and utterly drained by this life, this book is absolutely, 100 percent for you. There are millions of people who struggle daily with these very questions.

I want you to finally be unchained, with no restrictions on what you can do. There will be nothing standing in your way. *Regardless of your circumstances, past decisions, current struggles, or whatever, you will be set free from all of these.* That's my guarantee. You will be unleashed to live out your fullest potential. You will shine so bright that those around you will marvel at your energy, presence, and passion for life.

You will be what I have always called a world changer. The problem is many have stopped dreaming. This life has squashed down their ambitions and drive to accomplish goals. Their dreams are no longer big and apparent but small and hardly seen—so far away-seeming that they are forgotten.

When dreams dissipate, a sense of hopelessness and helplessness sets in. Life becomes miserable and unfulfilling. Life becomes a daily task performed with little passion. Personally, I do not want to see anyone experience these feelings of hopelessness.

My aim is to deliver my heart on a platter for you: to be an open book, to lay myself bare for everyone to see. My knowledge and wisdom will be exposed to those who are willing to listen.

By way of structure, in this book I've focused on Ten Authentic Habits—each one a chapter—that will help you discover the authentic you. As you explore each authentic habit—each chapter—take the opportunity to apply it to your life. The ten authentic habits build on each other. Through them, you will uncover levels of strength, happiness, contentment, and understanding that you might have never experienced before.

Over and over, I share my heart with you by using my past experiences to illustrate the journey you have ahead. How could I expect you to find your authentic self if I were not being completely authentic with you? Authenticity is my key ingredient for success in this book. All of the stories—however pungent or even sometimes, on the surface, *near-unbelievable*, are 100 percent factual. I experienced and lived them, and they brought me here.

Be absolutely present in the moment as you read. The overarching idea for this book is that it not be read once, a quick read and forgotten, but be a practical self-help book that will require effort to absorb and practice.

A strong level of self-development can be painstaking. But please, be patient with yourself and the process you have ahead in this book. Be mentally in the moment, choose to take the hard path and search out the answers you seek. More importantly, find the life you seek. An abundant life full of passion and purpose. Let us do this together, as you are not alone in this process of discovering the authentic you. The new you awaits you.

Foundation

The purpose for existence

> The rain came down, the streams rose,
> and the winds blew and beat against
> that house; yet it did not fall, because
> it had its foundation on the rock.
>
> —*Matthew the Apostle*

I have lived two lives: one with a weak foundation and the second with a strong foundation. My first life was the first eighteen years of my life: June 1, 1983, to July 15, 2001.

In my first life, I was lost, with no direction or sense of purpose. But you would not know it from the outside, looking in. I had a loving family, a close inner circle of friends, and my work ethic allowed me to get good at pretty much whatever I put my attention to. That was primarily athletics, as I did not pay attention to academics. I felt empty inside. I had no real vision of my purpose or my life going forward. I lived day to day. I could not see myself beyond the present. The pain in my life experiences, I was shoving down so deep I did not realize it was even there. My heart hurt, but I did not know why. I was a hardened young man with a fake, tough exterior. I needed help. Yet I did not even realize it. I felt like something was missing. What? I lacked any purpose in life, therefore felt passionless about life.

I was born June 1, 1983, at Hoag Hospital in Newport Beach in Orange County, California, between LA and San Diego. This was the beginning of my first life and the start of my journey to finding my strong foundation. My parents divorced when I was too young to remember. My mother said I was roughly two years old. My parents were polar opposites—both amazing people, but they lived two different lives. Despite similar values and morals, they had radically different lifestyles. I am incredibly grateful for both of them and learned multiple lessons from both. I would not be the man I am without both. I love Mom and Dad so much. I appreciate them beyond words.

My mom, an unbelievably amazing person, was always positive and optimistic—always one to try to do the right thing. A huge network of people loved and supported her. I would not call her a helicopter mom, but she was always there, whether I liked it or not. Always involved in my life. Always in my corner, ready to fight for me. Just writing these words brings a level of emotion; I cherish and appreciate her even more. I think you understand what kind of woman my mother was to me while I was growing up: one who loved unconditionally and relentlessly fought for her kids. I love you, Mom. I do not tell you enough. You are the best mom a son could ask for. After having two kids of my own, I know that even more. There is nothing I would not do for my kids. Thank you for the example of how I should unfailingly love my kids.

My dad was also an unbelievably amazing person as I was growing up. Likewise, extremely positive and optimistic, he was loved by everyone who knew him for being a fun-loving guy. Always having the best intentions, he was extremely kind to all around him. The defining difference between them was my dad's struggle with alcohol addiction. As with other addicts, the alcohol took first place for many years. I always wanted to spend time with my dad, but alcohol confiscated that spot. Even when we did spend time together, it would be at an arcade next to a bar. Unlike my mom, my dad did not set the best example. I just wanted my dad to be there for me, to be present in my life. I looked up to him tremendously. He was my dad. How could I not want to be like him?

I do not want to make my dad out to be the villain because he is absolutely not. He struggled, just like most people. Unfortunately, that struggle affected me. But that is long ago now. Thankfully, he's been sober for many decades. He is incredible, truly a one-of-a-kind person. One of the things my father taught me without trying (by setting an opposite example) is to be present in my kids' lives. Because of that longing I had, growing up, I told myself at a young age I would be a different dad. I would not be absent from my kids' lives if I was fortunate enough to have kids. That is a huge thing for me. Dad, I love you. I am incredibly thankful that you have come full circle. I am proud of you.

My parents met and fell in love in high school. They got married right after their senior graduation at only eighteen years old. They apparently had their whole graduating class of roughly three hundred people at their wedding. From what my mom states, my dad treated her like royalty the first ten of their twelve years of marriage. That's no surprise, as my dad loved my mom more than anything. He still reminds me of it to this day. Unfortunately, years eleven and twelve of their marriage were crazy. My dad went from partying on weekends, which my mom was partaking of, to partying every day.

At the time, he worked for Orange County, California, as a supervisor for a team. It began innocuously. To celebrate a hard day's work, he would take the boys out for drinks and food. My mom wasn't so happy about this since the bills were a couple thousand dollars. As I stated, my dad is extremely kind and generous. Unfortunately, they could not afford these generous bills my dad piled up. People say when you drink, you become more of who you are inside. Well, my dad became extremely generous and kind and loving when he drank. That's probably why everyone loved him. Sounds like a good friend to have. Unfortunately, it was just at Mom's and my expense.

As I previously stated, my parents got a divorce when I was roughly two years old. The straw that broke the camel's back was when my dad set up a drug deal at our house in Costa Mesa, California. Apparently, he came home, acting a little strange and nervous. Then he told my mom and me to get into the bedroom and not come out until he said the coast was clear. My mom dug in a little bit and came to find out my dad had a briefcase full of cocaine he was trying to sell. He was not an active drug dealer, but he was a wild man, looking to make some extra money. That was it; my mom gave him an ultimatum: get sober or we were leaving. My dad continued his party life.

As you can see, I did not know what it looked like to have a "whole family." For the purpose of my story, when I say, "whole family," I mean kids who had parents that were still together and in love, with neighborhood friends and a home to grow up in. I also realize that, unfortunately, divorce and unhappiness is prevalent in families. All that said, stability was the furthest thing from my childhood.

That is something I always desired, growing up, but never knew. In my mind my dad was the cool guy who let me swear, stay up late, watch inappropriate movies, and pretty much do whatever I wanted as long as I begged him enough, or if he was drinking (which was all the time). I remember him teaching me how to pour his morning beers before he drove me to school and went to his job. But I was a clever child, who also knew how to work my parents to get my way.

You could imagine as a child I wanted to be with my dad; he was cool with letting me pretty much have unlimited boundaries. Bear in mind, I was only in elementary school, and he let me do almost anything I wanted. As a young boy, it's hard to compete with a dad like that. I am trying to paint a picture of the two very distinct parents I had, growing up. That is important to know, considering they were my biggest influences. It really is true what they say: you mimic your role models, which as a child is usually your parents.

After the divorce I lived with my mom for the next nine years. In my mom's words, "It was just the two of us against the world." My mom has always been my biggest advocate, someone I could count on, who always took the time to make me feel loved and wanted. I love you tremendously. Thanks, Momma! Back to the story.

After my parents split up when I was two, my mom and I spent a few years on the run from my dad—going from apartment to apartment, trying to stay away from him and his crazy lifestyle. From what my mom tells me, he was making bad decisions left and right. Also, he was angry that my mom had left him. He wanted to get back together. My mom, doing what was best for us, wanted to start over without my dad in the picture. That is, until he decided to get help. Thank God! He was a wild man when he was living that life.

Though I was young, I remember we financially struggled compared to the typical Orange County life. Also, we bounced all over Orange County. We never owned a home; I naturally felt a little jealous of those families around me that did. As a child, I would see friends, television personalities, and people around me with a "whole family." I was angry, envious, whatever you want to call it. I wanted a home with parents who loved each other and friends I knew for longer than a couple years. I always felt like that kid who moved into a neighborhood and was gone in the next year.

Do not get me wrong, I was never a loner—just the opposite. Always the center of attention: cracking jokes, instigating bad behavior. And extremely athletic. That never hurts if you are trying to fit into new circles. Anytime we moved to another city, though I would make friends with no problem, there was always a restlessness in me. Looking back, I realize it was that restlessness that made me act out as the center of attention and get into trouble. I believe there were two main reasons I was a troubled child: I was angry about the divorce and unhappy about my dad not being in my life.

Actually, in preschool I was expelled for hitting another child with a wooden gun. Mind you, this was 1987. I'm not sure for what exact reason I did hit the child, but it reflected my anger issue. Even at that age, I would inevitably get in a fight with anyone who stood up to me, especially if they mentioned my mom or dad. Back then, it was pretty typical to hear "your mama" jokes. I did not like those one bit. Any mention of my family brought up red flags. I was an angry child.

After Dad got better . . . but not completely sober . . . he would pick me up from my mom's house. I imagined us as father and son hanging out together. But it was rarely about me. It was about my dad's agenda. If he was not drinking, then he was about to and we were on his schedule. I remember wanting more of him. Wanting to do stuff together. And he always liked the idea but would say, "Maybe tomorrow or next week." You can see where I am going. We rarely did anything I wanted to but stuck to what he felt at the time.

I am still thankful, though, my dad did teach me some good habits by example. I was an observant child. From watching him, I learned about the small details—discipline and a work ethic. You would think those are qualities an alcoholic would not have, but my dad did. I have to say again, thank you, Dad! Though reckless from drinking, he was far from the stereotypical slob. By trade a general contractor, he was a perfectionist at his craft, a hard worker, and extremely disciplined in his daily habits. Still, through all my observing, I thought maybe the reason I was unsettled was I needed my dad to be involved in my life and simply spend quality time with his son. I was desperate to get his attention.

When I was around six, my mom got remarried to my dad's best man from her first wedding. It seems random and kind of funny that my dad's best man ended up being my stepdad. My dad did not think it was funny. Now we were adding a stepdad to the picture.

Let's just say, my stepdad and I didn't really get along. We had a lot of heated arguments. My stepdad meant well, but it was a difficult situation for him.

To make matters worse, my stepdad also had an alcohol problem. My living situation was getting more chaotic. My dad was open about drinking, which was why he was a nut job, drinking. My stepdad, on the other hand, was a closet drinker. He tried to keep it a secret. Remember what I said about people who drink: the real self comes out. My stepdad would get angry. Never physical with us, but I distinctly remember my mom and stepdad battling it out on frequent occasions, exchanging a lot of loud, hurtful words. And they fought over the absolute stupidest things. We would be on route to a destination. They would fight over what was the best street to take to get us there the quickest. I remember that fight occurred almost daily.

My stepdad tried to father me, but I was not having it. Anything he said to me was contradictory to my father, and I refused to listen. And it's not like he was asking a lot of me. It might be, "clean your room," "do the dishes" or "take out the trash": basic chores. But to me at the time, I realize now, I was defending my dad. I will admit, I was quite hard-headed. Even after all the difficult times I had with my stepdad, I still loved and appreciated him. I have a lot of one-liners stuck in my head from him. Positive one-liners. Thank you for doing your best. I know it was not always easy.

Right after my mom and stepdad got married, they had my first brother. Then my second. I have to say, with all the chaos, that was a light in my life. I always wanted a brother, let alone two brothers. It was amazing! In my mind, it was great to finally see something go my way. But there was a decent age gap and different upbringing that made it a little difficult to connect with them. I love my brothers so much. I am so incredibly thankful for them. As time has gone on, we've been able to dive deeper into our individual relationships. That one is still a work in progress.

I had visitation rights with my dad on random weekends. It was not as consistent as I would have liked, but at least I got to see him. Sometimes he would come over drunk, and my mom would turn him away. That would piss him off; he would get in the car and burn tread on the way out. I didn't fully understand what was going on. I remember being so excited about seeing my dad, then just watching him storm off, furious. I wasn't sure if it was something I did, or who knows. I was only around seven.

I was seeing an anger therapist. To be honest, I do not remember too much of what was said. I'm not sure it even helped. The therapist would try to get emotions out of me, but I was a tank. Even at a young age, I slowly but surely cultivated a hardened heart. It's hard being young and not knowing how to process your emotions. When you're a kid, it is a challenge. I can see why kids act out the way they do. In most cases it falls back to their parents and upbringing. There are a ton of broken families out there with similar stories to mine.

One day I was hanging out with friends in the neighborhood, rollerblading, which was popular in the '80s and '90s. One of my friends stormed over to me and told me my mom was on the phone with someone, crying profusely. I stormed over to our apartment in a panic. Apparently, my mom was on the phone with her mom. She'd just found out her younger brother, my uncle, who was only in his thirties, all of a sudden died in his sleep of a blood clot. That was devastating. Anything that affected my mom affected me. My mom was my anchor. That day, I will never forget. My mom was always such a light, but that's when I noticed her light become a little dimmer. In my eyes, my mom is still the brightest light you will ever meet.

My uncle was exceptionally tall, roughly seven feet. He had a huge, warm smile, and he was exceptionally kind to me and, really, everyone around him—truly a gentle giant. He would always hoist me onto his shoulders and run me around the house, which was so fun because he had to bend his head down every time he walked through a doorway. So, I was almost ten feet tall on his shoulders. He was such a kind man. I did not get to know him as long as I would have liked, but I am thankful for the time I had with him. I did not have too many positive influences in my life, but he was definitely a positive role model. Thank you, Uncle. See you someday again.

Longing for my dad, I realized I wanted to live with him, so I pushed my mom for years till she eventually reluctantly said OK. She knew she could not play both roles. Once again, I was moving to another city.

I was about nine when I moved from Mission Viejo, California, to Big Bear, California, a completely different environment, roughly two hours from my mom, which could not have been easy for her. Mission Viejo is about ten minutes from the beach, and Big Bear is in a small mountain village, roughly two hours away from the coast, at an elevation of almost nine thousand feet. At that time it had a population of a little over a thousand. Compared to Mission Viejo— at sea level, with a hundred thousand inhabitants—that is a pretty big change in environment.

After I moved in, I thought to myself: *I finally get to be with my dad, the cool guy who lets me do what I want, but most importantly we can finally be together as father and son bonding.* This was not to be. I learned quickly that it was not how I imagined. Yes, we were together every day, but, as I stated before, my dad had an agenda that came before me. I quietly reflected maybe I was asking too much of him, or we did not have enough to do, living in a town without much to offer.

At this time, Big Bear was a small mountain community, with few fun things to do for kids. We had an arcade, one movie theater, a candy shop, one bobsled ride, a ski resort (snowboarding did not exist yet), and lots of woodsy trails for hiking. One of the things I found most enjoyable to do with my friends was explore in the woods. We ran into a lot of wildlife. It's crazy, looking back, remembering not wearing shoes, even sandals. We literally just hiked out into the woods barefoot. Also, we got into trouble, breaking things—just being boys. That was fun! That is pretty much what I did, plus the daily trips down to the liquor store. I remember always asking my dad to go to the resort to learn how to ski, but he always gave his standard response: "It was a good idea, Son. We'll go do that. But not today, maybe tomorrow or next week." We lived there for almost three years, and we never did end up going to the ski resort. I learned that my dad had specific time slots for me. These time slots added up to a maximum of a couple hours. Hence, that explains why we unfailingly went to the arcade, movies, or candy shop, or on a bobsled ride. He was always drinking and smoking, never truly present.

Most parents think their kids do not fully understand what decisions they make as a parent, but let me tell you, they most definitely do. Kids, at the end of the day, want to mimic their parents. That's what I started to do: be my dad, the cool guy. Not like I started drinking, but I wanted to be the life of the party. That was about the time I started stealing and really creating havoc in school, or wherever I could. Keep in mind, I was only nine years old—stealing, ditching school, getting in fights, getting suspended, etc. I was only following what my dad taught me through his example.

My dad and I took multiple trips to the local liquor store to grab some groceries. I remember him wearing these sweatpants that had a collar at the bottom to catch things he would stuff down his pants. I will never forget the first time I saw him steal. I looked at him as he was stuffing small liquor bottles into the cuffs. I knew what he was doing, but I didn't know why. He looked at me with a big smile and said something like, "Shhh, getting some goodies for later." I remember thinking that this would be our little secret. Little did my dad know I looked up to him and this would set a bad example for my future choices. My dad made one small choice to steal that day in front of me, and in return I learned to steal, be dishonest, and ultimately break the law. Of course, at the end of the day, we all have a choice to make, but my dad did not give me the best model.

A couple times a month, depending on the weather and how I was feeling, my dad would drive me over to my mom's. Since we lived in the mountains, it snowed a lot during the winter. And to make matters worse, I experienced extreme motion sickness when I was younger. So, pretty much every time we went down and up the mountain, I got sick. For that reason, on multiple occasions I tried to get out of going to see my mom. Personally, I hated getting sick in the car. Plus, my dad had a 1980s Volkswagen camper van that swayed all over the place. Plus, my dad didn't have much of a fear factor, so he drove well over the speed limit. Plus, he drank. My dad was a functioning alcoholic at this point. So he went at it from morning until night. Every day.

On one particular occasion, we were headed back from my mom's to Big Bear. I was roughly nine. Outside, an extreme snowstorm obscured all visibility, and my dad had a few drinks in his system. We'd just made it safely back into town. Granted, it was difficult to see, but out of nowhere a man hit the hood of our truck and was flung into the air over the truck. It happened so quickly it was difficult to process. My dad pulled over and went out to help the guy. He also called the police and paramedics. They came, and thankfully the man was OK, with minor injuries. But my dad was not. Arrested for his third DUI, he was taken to jail. Then I was up in Big Bear at the local county jail, hanging out with the police. They were extremely kind to me, giving me unlimited goodies out of the vending machine. That was awesome! They called my dad's mom to come pick me up. Because of the snowstorm I was at the station for a few hours. By the time my grandmother picked me up, it was something like 2:00 a.m.

Now, after spending almost three years up in Big Bear and in three separate homes, we moved to Fountain Valley, California. I was about eleven, halfway through my fifth grade. Once again, we were uprooting, moving. Resettling away from my friends, again. We moved to my grandma Barrena's house. Now, my grandma Barrena took over the role as parent since my dad did not do the best job. I would consider my dad's mom, my grandmother, to be my second mom. She was an incredible person.

My grandmother was 100 percent Cuban. Cuba was where my dad was born as well: Havana. They moved to the United States when Fidel Castro took office. My dad was young: I believe he was roughly seven. To even describe my grandmother is difficult, she was so special to me. She taught me so much about life. She spent time with me. She was my missing parent. She taught me all about Cuban food, my heritage, hard work, discipline, and passion. More importantly, she helped me process what my dad was going through with his addiction. She would affirm that my dad meant well, but he was sick and needed help, but the choice to get better was his. I love my grandmother so much. She was a successful entrepreneur—a clothing designer, seamstress, and business owner. She owned a couple of clothing lines back in the '80s and '90s. She ended up selling her businesses for a good profit and relocated near Spokane, Washington.

Needless to say, it was nice to live in a more stable environment with my grandmother present. Naturally, we lived with my grandfather too. He was an ornery and angry man. He acted like he never really liked me, so we did not spend much time talking or really doing anything together. I was surprised my grandmother was even with him, as he was her opposite. Contrasting my very positive and optimistic grandmother, my grandfather was negative and pessimistic. I guess, opposites really do attract.

On a couple of occasions when I got into mischief, my grandpa grabbed me by the hair and dragged me to my room. He was old school in that way. I did not mind getting punished by him, as I thought I deserved it for the naughty things I was doing. I would light glue on fire in the backyard or shoot birds with my BB guns. On one occasion, I shot and killed a toucan bird, which I called the Fruit Loops bird, in our backyard. We found out later, it was a pet that had escaped from a neighbor's home. Unfortunately, the neighbor never found the bird . . . I wonder why. As I said, I was always getting into trouble. On a positive note, my grandfather was highly intelligent. He would build sophisticated things from scratch. Some of the things he built were planes, cars, and radios. Pretty impressive man when you think about it.

It was nice to live in a home that was practically across the street from school. I was able to ride my bike. I was halfway through my fifth-grade year, meeting new friends and getting on my teacher's nerves—always the kid who was clowning around. My teacher thought I had a learning disorder since I would not pay attention. I really disliked school and the structure of it. I just wanted to hang out and play sports. I lacked the attention span to focus in class, primarily because I did not care for school. Not surprisingly, my dad put no emphasis on education. Since he did not care, I did not care.

My fifth-grade teacher tried everything to get me to pay attention. One thing my teacher did was take a cardboard box she homemade; then she placed me in it, directly in the front of the class. She cut out a little hole in the front so I could see her teach the class. This obviously brought a spectacle to the classroom since I was the only one in a box. This was 1995, a time when things like this were permitted. But that did not stop me from poking holes in the side of the box so I could see my friends, to keep cracking jokes. It was quite apparent my teacher hated me. I was that difficult a child. I had a problem with authority. I had a problem with anything that was not exactly what I wanted to do at the moment.

One day my mom came for a surprise visit. When she saw what the teacher had done, putting me in the box, she went on an absolute rampage—perfectly livid, she was candid with the teacher, principal, and anyone else involved. My teacher never did anything like that again. She even transferred me to another class after the incident. My mom was a force to be reckoned with. She was always in my corner, fighting for me. I loved it that my mom loved me so much. She was always such a shining example of how a parent should be towards her children. I only wanted my dad to have that same love for me. No matter what my mom did to show me how much she loved me, it could not replace the void, where my dad was not involved in my life.

After the school incident, it was recommended for me to go see a specialist for attention deficit disorder. They thought that's what I had. I ended up being diagnosed with ADD and prescribed the central nervous system stimulant Ritalin. After a couple months on Ritalin, we ended up stopping the medication since it made me even more hyperactive. I personally believe I did not have ADD. I just really disliked school since my role model put no emphasis on it. I put zero percent effort into school. Anything else I set my mind to learn— like sports, artwork, crafts, woodworking, building relationships, or anything else I really enjoyed, I quickly excelled in. But I put zero effort forward. I could imagine from my parents' perspective, looking from the outside in, that I needed help. Reflecting now, I believe I did need help but *not* the kind they were offering: I needed a father figure. I needed my role model to step up and be the man I knew he could be.

Paradoxically, my dad seemed to be getting worse. He was drinking just as much as ever, which was all the time: breakfast, lunch, dinner. But after well over a decade of abuse, it seemed to finally be taking a toll. He ended up becoming diabetic, in and out of rehab. On multiple occasions, I found him in a diabetic coma. I would have to give him a sugar pill, call the paramedics, and wait for him to be resuscitated. I recall one time, after I spent a weekend at my mom's house, my mom brought me back to my dad's. We found him on the kitchen floor, completely naked in his own pee and vomit. I was pretty numb in life at this point, but that incident had an effect on me. I could not quite pinpoint my feelings. I was twelve, by then. I was not sure if it was shame for my dad or fear of losing him. I stopped calling him by the name I had always called him, "Dad." I began calling him by his first name and barely acknowledging his presence. That quickly took a toll on my dad. I saw how much it really hurt him. In a way, I was trying to get back at him for the pain he'd caused me.

Shortly after that incident in 1995, my dad finally decided to quit alcohol. Forever. He did it cold turkey: just stopped. Never went to Alcoholics Anonymous or rehab. He's been 100 percent sober from that day on. On the one hand, it was a miracle. On the other, my dad made a choice. I believe he did it not to lose a son, his only child—debatably, the rare good thing in his life. That was the first time I truly witnessed and experienced my dad's love for me. I could not have been prouder of him. I always knew my dad loved me, but at that instant I saw the feeling in action. For the first time. There are not many greater loves than a parent for a child. Now, that is a deep love.

At this point, I was in the middle of my sixth-grade year at Northcutt Elementary in Fountain Valley. For one of the only times I could remember, I took a deep breath and enjoyed my dad's sobriety, extremely grateful to have a coherent dad. I had never had that. It was a new experience. I do remember in that year my dad being more present in my life. We spent many beautiful times together, but that would come to a quick halt because of my next bad choice.

Towards the end of the school year, I took my dog on a walk down the street to a local superstore. I attempted to steal twelve music CDs and ended up getting caught on the way out. A couple of police officers were waiting for me outside with handcuffs. They took me to the back of the store and called my dad. When my dad and grandmother arrived, my dad was livid. I was terrified. My grandmother was in tears. I knew I'd done something bad, but my only regret in that instant was getting caught. The police allowed my dad to take me home. There, he told me to get straight to my room, where I stayed for a couple hours to think about what I'd done. I honestly did not have remorse. I was up there, just listening to music on the radio. My dad came in to say good night. I was in bed, and the lights were off. My dad sat at my bedside, put his head down, and started to weep. I had never seen my dad cry, let alone weep. With what little breath he had, he mustered a few words. My dad said, "Son, let's not tell your mother about this. She will make you move away from me." I never again heard him cry.

Well, as you can imagine, my mother ended up finding out. Just a short couple of months later my mother received a call from the courthouse, telling her that I was due in court. She was surprised and extremely upset, as you can imagine. Almost immediately I was forced to move back with my mom, stepdad, and brothers. Once again, in the summer of 1996, I was forced to move to another city, Mission Viejo. Forced to start all over at another school. The biggest gut check was, I finally got a sober dad, who started to get involved in my life, but had to move away. That was painful.

Though sad and angry about this development, I ended up deciding to make the most of it. I knew there was no way my mom would let me move back with my dad. I am sure she blamed some of my bad behavior on him. He absolutely was the biggest influence in my life, but I was the one making the bad choices. It was 100 percent my fault.

Thankfully, since I had moved around a lot, I was quite accustomed to making new friends. I never struggled in that department. Day one in seventh grade, I met a group of boys who were into skateboarding. Naturally, that became my next sport. I ended up joining the skateboard crew. Back then, skateboarders were seen as pothead druggies. Basically, we were taken for hoodlums. Well, that's exactly what we were. Before long, I got quite good at skateboarding. I was also quite the party animal. In seventh grade I started to smoke weed, smoke cigarettes, and drink alcohol regularly. No one forced me to. I was more of an influencer and leader than led by others.

The way I looked at it, drugs and partying seemed fun, and they were. So I did what I enjoyed most. I was living day to day:

attempting to enjoy life to the fullest, as I called it. Drugs were the beginning of my spiral downward. On a positive note, this was one of the first times I really learned discipline and a work ethic. I wanted to get good at skateboarding and I did. The only way to get good at anything in life is to put in the work and be consistently disciplined. I skateboarded every day and all the time. Almost every thought I had was consumed by skateboarding. And by skateboarding, I mean street skating. I was big into ledges, manuals, stairs, gaps, and handrails. I also learned about a creative side I didn't know existed. Whether it was my brain maturing and realizing this for the first time, I got to see how creative I could be on a skateboard. It was really fun!

Side note—one of the professional skateboarders I looked up to at the time was Ronnie Creager. He was one of my favorites because of his creativity and style while skateboarding. Oddly enough, I met him later in life on a golf course. We ended up becoming good buddies and still keep in touch today. Kind of awesome how your childhood heroes can become your friends later in life. Back to my story.

But I still found it difficult to focus on school. All I wanted to do was skateboard and party. So in the seventh-grade year, along with getting multiple citations for misconduct and goofing off in class, I fell behind. The school decided it would be in my best interest to be expelled and try a different school. Therefore, in eighth grade, I attended a new school, nearby. It's no surprise that at this one, I got on the teacher's nerves. Since it was a different school, I also felt like I had to start over, again. It was just a city away, fairly close to my previous school, so I still kept the same friends, give or take a couple.

I was able to make tons of new friends at my new school as well. Especially since I had the reputation of being a good skater, I instantly fit in with the cool kids, if you know what I mean. In eighth grade is when I began to take a real interest in the opposite sex. I was a little girl crazy! But, what fourteen-year-old boy isn't? I remember really enjoying eighth grade, what with being good at skateboarding, having tons of friends, and seeming apparently to be liked by the ladies. Plus, I knew how to party, and that I did, harder than the previous year.

It was 1998. I started to compete in skateboarding in the California Amateur Skateboard League. That was the first time I experienced the competitive arena of a sport. To be honest, I enjoyed it but did not really put in the effort to do my best. I just kind of coasted through competitions. In some I finished well; some I did not. I did not really care either way. Towards the end of the year a select few had a chance to compete in the finals. I skated well enough to place in the top five for the state, with one of my good buddies taking the first spot. Again, I did not really care. It was cool. At the time, skateboarding to me was not about the competition but about the artistry, creativity, and style a skater brought to the table. Plus, I was probably slightly hung over from the night before. I was doing plenty of partying in my spare time.

Meanwhile, homelife was decent. It was much more stable than I remember the first several years of my life being. My dad, still sober, ended up moving out of state to a fairly small city called Cheney, just outside Spokane, Washington. It was sad to see him relocate out of state. But it did not bug me much, now that I had skateboarding and a new group of friends to preoccupy me. Living with my mom, stepdad, and brothers was fine by me. I did not spend a lot of time at home. Home was basically a bed to sleep in and food to eat. Though living in upscale Orange County, we were on the lower-income spectrum, while not homeless. We did not participate in the stereotypical Orange County lifestyle. We found a program for affordable housing. The program was simple—real-estate agents had properties to sell, so we staged their homes with our furniture. In short, we got a drastic rent reduction, moving into a home with our furniture staged for potential buyers to come, with little to no advance notice, and view the property for purchase. A home typically sold in three to six months. Then we moved out. I personally really liked it since we got to see new environments, and at this point, I was quite used to moving. So it was a natural fit.

Well into my ninth-grade year at Laguna Hills High, I was still constantly a troublemaker—ditching class, getting into fights, and indulging in other misconduct. For me, it was a way of life since I'd been that way my entire life from the example I learned early on. I was still skateboarding a lot, partying even more often—doing nothing noteworthy besides skateboarding. I had no real sense of purpose or foundation in my life.

In April 1999, I decided to make one of the poorest choices to date. We were in the middle of our lunch hour at school in a central area where everyone hung out. One of my friends brought a huge pack of black cat firecrackers. There must have been at least fifty. A few of us were standing in a circle. It was a gloomy day and a little cold, so we were all huddled up closer than normal. My friend proceeded to show us the firecrackers and dared one of us to light them. I did not even hesitate. I pulled out the lighter in my pocket that I was playing with, lit the fuse, and walked away like nothing had happened. Now, just a few days prior were the Columbine shootings. As one of the first school mass shootings, it was completely tragic. But I was a careless fifteen-year-old boy, making another poor choice at almost every turn.

As soon as the firecrackers started to go off, everyone at the school panicked. It sounded like gunfire. People were dropping to the floor, running, shouting, crying—which makes sense because a shooting just happened a few days prior. They thought this was one too. I'd been thoughtless and careless. Within minutes tons of law enforcement, SWAT, helicopters, and paramedics arrived. After the first hour everyone realized it was a false alarm, then started investigating. Who was behind it all? I'd been in a small group of friends when I lit the firecrackers. I and two others had casually walked away like nothing happened, but two of my friends decided to run. Our group was discovered as the source of the incident.

Over the next few days we all got interrogated. We were all locked tight on our story, but one of our friends ended up caving. I got caught. I was immediately expelled from the school district. Once again, my mom came to my rescue. My mom is relentless. She was a titan for me. She went back and forth with the principal and finally cut a deal. The deal was that I would finish my ninth-grade year and the first half of my tenth-grade year at another high school. As long as I maintained a certain grade average and remained on good behavior, I'd be allowed to return to Laguna Hills High. Sure enough, I did not want to let my mom down. I ended up fulfilling my requirements and returned to Laguna Hills High.

I was still skateboarding every day and getting extremely good. Good enough to go pro one day. I got my first sponsor, a board shop, and then ended up accumulating some other sponsors along the way. My friends and I were making skateboarding footage on a regular basis. Back in the late '90s we had to use large camcorders . . . much less convenient than today's smartphones.

Along with street skating came trespassing, vandalism, and breaking into private property. On almost a daily basis we were running from the cops or being chased by helicopters off roofs that were fun to skateboard or gymnasiums that were fun to break into to skate. We even broke into a church to skateboard the wooden handrail in the gym. Basically, we did not abide by many rules. If someplace was good to skate, we would make it happen. My friends and I were arrested on multiple occasions for these offenses. But it came with the territory, so we were used to it. The thrill of running from the cops was pretty fun too. Hopping backyard fences and hiding in bushes. The funniest was being chased by helicopters. Typically, you would hear them coming; then the police would start to speak to you on their intercom, and we would all scatter, on the run. The helicopter would pick a group of kids or one kid to follow, and that inevitably ended up being the kid who got caught. It was a fun time to skateboard. Not what it is today, with skateboarding being in the Olympics and competitions being held all around the world.

As time went on, I was partying more and more. It was the year 2000. I was in my junior year of high school, doing more and more drugs. Drinking more frequently. I'd gotten into ecstasy and cocaine as well towards the beginning of ninth grade. They were big back in the late '90s. But I was going downhill fast. I started to notice that I wanted to skateboard less and party more. That is when things got worse for me. I fell behind in school from carelessness and lack of attendance. I skipped a lot of my homework and school assignments. Ended up having a meeting with my guidance counselor, who suggested I go to a continuation school to catch up. It would allow me to graduate on time. If I stayed at Laguna Hills High School, I would be held back a year.

My mom and I decided in favor of the continuation school, an at-home program. I loved it! I only had to go to a brick-and-mortar school once a week for roughly thirty minutes to drop off my schoolwork and pick up my new assignment. Which was great. I was able to pick my own curriculum, depending on what I wanted to study. I wish I had found this school sooner. I got a job, working nearly full time, got my schoolwork done at my own pace, skateboarded with my buddies, and partied all night. My mom was giving me a lot of freedom right then. As long as I put on a good face for her and said all the right things, she let me do pretty much whatever I wanted. I was like a little adult. But all the bad decisions were going to catch up to me quickly. I found myself staying up later and later with my friends. I was an instigator. Some days we would be out till 2:00 a.m. On one particular night, we were hanging out at a park down the street from my neighborhood—not doing anything out of the normal, just smoking some weed and drinking some alcohol. It was pretty late. I am not sure the exact time. We ended up getting arrested for being drunk in public and possession of marijuana. The cops handcuffed us, put us in the back of the cop car, and took us home. My mom was mortified in tears; my brothers were shocked, and my stepdad expected it.

I remember waking up the next day, and it being a big thing to my mom based on her reaction. To me, it was just another day. I had zero remorse. I just went about my business as if nothing ever happened. At this stage, I realize, looking back, I was a hardened individual. Except for my friends, partying, and skateboarding, I did not really care about anything.

The only really positive influence in my life besides my mom was Kelly Hart. Only Kelly, of all my friends, was passionate about getting as good as possible at skateboarding without the drug use. Since he didn't party, he regularly invited me over to his house to skate. Shining onto his driveway, he had flood lamps—with rails, ramps, and ledges for skating. For several hours, until late in the evening, we skated, and then his parents ordered in some pizza as we watched skate videos. We never did anything mischievous, which was abnormal for me. It's not a shocker that Kelly ended up becoming a well-known professional skateboarder, as he put in the work without the extracurricular party life, unlike me. Looking at the announcement in 2020 that he'd become the Ricta Wheels and Mob Grip team manager, I felt myself swell with pride, thinking of what he has accomplished. That is an example of two very talented skateboarders with different priorities. In those early days, Kelly was a good skateboarder, *but I was better*. Yet Kelly made it happen, and I did not.

Thankfully, I was still getting out there, skateboarding—the one positive thing I seemed to be doing in my life. With skateboarding comes injuries. I have sprained my wrist and ankles too many times to count. I have broken roughly thirteen bones: wrists, arms, shoulders, ribs, feet, and ankles. Oh, the life of a skateboarder. Especially one who liked to do stairs, gaps, and handrails.

On one particular day in June 2001, I was feeling good, excited about summer. I had just turned eighteen, and now I could buy cigarettes legally. It was right before my junior year of high school ended, so no more school since the summer was about to begin. At that moment, life was good. My buddies and I were skating on this handrail that went down beside six steps. For those of you who know street skating, I was doing a switch noseslide to regular out. Nothing particularly fancy. But as soon as you landed, you went off the curb. If you know skateboarding, that makes it a little bit trickier. And as soon as you went off the curb, you were right in between two parking stall curbs. You know, those things that stop you from running into the curb with your car. Well, I was a perfectionist with my skateboarding. If I did not stomp the trick straight onto the bolts with no body movement and perfect style, at least in my mind, I would not be satisfied.

In this particular incident, it was no different. I landed it multiple times in a row, but in my mind it was not perfect. Skaters know this feeling. Plus, I wanted to see how many times I could do it in a row. I believe it was my sixth time in a row when I stomped the trick but instantly jumped off my skateboard; I then jumped forward and wrapped my left foot around the curb. Instantly broke my left foot and knew it, based on past experiences. Knew it right away. I was pretty bummed, considering I had already landed the trick multiple times. I'd just been letting my ego get in the way. To make matters worse, summer was about to begin, and now I was going to be in a cast. Considering that I was doing lots of partying and my only outlet from that bad behavior was skateboarding, it was the perfect storm for my doom.

Naturally, my mother came to take me to urgent care. Sure enough, I did break my foot in multiple places. Because of the swelling, they could not give me a cast for a few days. But the doctor did ask me if I was in pain, and I said, "Absolutely," which was a lie: I have a fairly high pain threshold—so, I've learned from all my injuries. In fact, I seem to have handled a large amount of pain over the years. But I knew if I told the doctor I was in pain, he'd give me some pain pills. Sounded like a good high to me. The doctor ended up prescribing me a bottle of Vicodin. Though I was not happy about breaking my foot, I was happy about the Vicodin. I was popping those things like candy. That, combined with weed and alcohol, made for what I thought was a good time. The bottle of Vicodin only lasted me a little over a week.

It was July 4, 2001, what I call my judgment day. I was about to go on a journey that was unforeseen and unlike anything I had ever experienced. It was going to be one of the most difficult experiences of my life. I was hanging out with my friends at my place, smoking some weed, drinking, and sniffing some coke. You might say we were celebrating the holiday, but it was a regular occurrence for us. Since we were at my place and my family was about to get home, we needed to leave. We ended up going down the street to what we called, "The Ditch." A secluded place in a large sewer drain ditch where my friends and I would hang out often.

It was on the side of a hill, covered by bushes and away from people. It was our go-to hangout for drinking, smoking weed, tagging, and rapping. Yes, my buddies and I did freestyle rap back in the day. My rap name was "Digest the Best." We had a few years of practice under our belts, and we were not that bad. A couple of my buddies knew how to beatbox fairly well, so we would all take turns, speaking poetry with our words. At least, it was that to us. The Ditch was also all graffitied up with our "tags," aka artwork. Plus, it was the meetup point for our nightly mischief.

By the time we arrived at The Ditch, it had just gotten dark. We were smoking weed and freestyle rapping. I was waiting for my turn to drop a dope rap, when I had a random thought. It was unlike any other I had ever had if not on any hallucinogen. I was sitting on The Ditch ledge, crouched over with my feet in front of me and my elbows on my legs with my hands together like you are about to pray—you know, in the position of getting ready to freestyle—when I thought to myself: *Let me try to make my hands melt together.*

Even then, I knew that was a strange thought. But I went along with it. So, with my hands together and eyes forward, sure enough, seconds later my hands melted together, forming the letter A; neon-green Christmas trees and Smurfs started to fly out of the center of the A towards my face. Realizing I'd just seen something unreal, I instantly jerked my body back. My heart rate dramatically increased as I started to have a panic attack. My friends, noticing my reaction, looked over at me. I completely downplayed the shocking situation by freestyling. My friends did not think much about it, as I kept to myself what had happened. But I was in full panic mode. I realized that I'd just hallucinated something—it was not really there. I was freaking out.

I was completely terrified about what I'd witnessed. So much so that I asked one of my buddies if he wanted to stay the night. I needed some level of comfort, which my buddy was hopefully going to provide. I was wrong. When we got back to my place later that night, I felt like I had a big secret to tell everyone, but I could not tell anyone or else I would give it power. My secret? I am losing my mind. I was not sure exactly why this was happening to me, but it was happening. We got into my room and settled into bed with the TV on.

My buddy was sleeping on the ground in a sleeping bag, and I was on my bed, watching TV. I had all of these skateboard posters on my wall. As I was watching TV, in the background all of the posters started to swirl on the wall. I was just trying to keep it together. After they stopped swirling, a couple of the posters became crystal clear. One was a swastika, and the other was the imperial eagle, another Nazi symbol. I instantly knew that whatever I was dealing with was extremely evil. I had never thought about those sorts of things before. *Such evil thoughts or images in my mind!* It was scary, to say the least.

At the same time I was seeing these horrifically evil symbols, I started to melt into my bed. Not really, but I was hallucinating. As I was melting into my bed, I felt pitchforks prodding at my back.

There were also hands feeling my back and pulling me down into my bed. Almost as if they were demons trying to take me down to hell. As you can imagine, I was terrified. But I kept it together enough to act like I was normal.

While I was mentally freaking out, I thought that this was karma for all the bad things I'd done; they were finally catching up to me. For those of you who do not know, when you are hallucinating, it feels 100 percent real. Obviously, it is not real, but it looks real, feels real, smells real, and any other sense that you may have. It is 100 percent convincing to you. There are positive hallucinations and negative ones. This was absolutely negative and a living nightmare. For the next twelve days, I felt like I was being put into a room to be tortured, with no escape and little hope.

I thought if I could go to bed, maybe I would wake up tomorrow and it would all be gone. Like it was a bad dream. Well, I barely got any sleep that night, as it was mental torture all night. After I woke up from what felt like a little nap, nothing got better. I knew then that something had control of my mind, but I did not know what it was. I went about my business, trying to forget about the huge elephant in the room that no one knew about but me. I was losing my mind. I needed help but had no clue where to begin.

This was the start of a twelve-day bad trip. I cannot tell you all the experiences I had during these twelve days, but it was my worst nightmare come to reality. I truly believed these bad things were happening to me because I was a bad person who only cared about himself. My desires. My wants. My needs. It finally all caught up to me.

It was only the second night of my horror story. I was in my room all alone. Trying to not completely lose my mind. I was constantly seeing the floor, walls, and ceiling swirl and close in on me—at times as if I were in a miniscule box. I could barely stand it. I got up and went down the hall to my mom and stepdad's room. It was roughly midnight. I opened the door and whispered, "Mom."

She answered, "Yes, sweetie?" I said, "I had a bad dream. Can I sleep next to you?" She said, "Absolutely." As she pulled the covers down for me to jump into bed, my stepdad woke up and said, "What? You want to hop into bed with us? Are you kidding me?" Well, thankfully he was tired and just fell straight back to sleep. I proceeded to hop into bed next to the person, my mom, I thought could provide me with the comfort I so desperately needed. I was terribly wrong.

Keep in mind, I was an eighteen-year-old—a teenager who believed he was bad to the bone. I was a rule breaker through and through. I was in trouble with the law. I was popular for skateboarding and being the life of the party. I was one of the leaders amongst my friends. I did not have the best relationship with my family, as I was too cool for school. That was the person I was. I believe God had to break me in order to restore me. I was also the person now asking to sleep in bed with his mommy. The one person who, I felt, added a sense of comfort. I was losing my mind, I needed comfort any way I could get it.

Once in bed, I was hoping to fall right asleep. Wrong again. Same thing as happened the previous night: I started to sink into the bed, with those pitchforks and hands trying to pull me down into the unknown abyss that played hell in my mind. Then I had a new experience. I started to levitate above the bed. Not for real. Hallucinating. But I found myself three inches from the roof of my mom's bedroom ceiling. I could practically smell that popcorn ceiling, as if it were just barely scraping my nose. This was the sort of night I had, all night. It was an extremely rough night, but once again, I got through it, barely.

As days went on, it became more difficult to hold it together. I was keeping this big secret to myself. I was losing my mind but believed I would find an answer that could help. About five days into my nightmare, I had a conversation with my mom in the car on the way to a friend's. I told her that these "bad dreams" were very persistent. I was still not telling my mom or anyone else the truth. I wanted to make sure this secret remained hush-hush. I believed if I told someone, people would look at me differently, not to mention try to lock me up. That was an ongoing thought and fear. I pictured myself in a white padded room, with a straitjacket hugging my body. Blood running down the walls. Spiders crawling over my body. For the rest of my life.

As I was telling my mom about these "bad dreams," I explained that I did not understand why. She proceeded to ask me if I had any more Vicodin. I told her I ran out a while ago. She was instantly concerned, as my mom has worked in the medical field, doing home care for the sick and elderly practically her whole life. Some of her clients had had experiences with situations similar to what I was describing. She right away told me that one of the side effects of overdosing on Vicodin was hallucinating. I instantly, for the first time since this nightmare began, started to feel like there was light at the end of the tunnel. I now knew what was making me hallucinate. My mom told me, based on when I stopped taking the pills, to give it a few days to allow the Vicodin to run through my system. And, she instructed me, consume a lot of water and healthy fluid to help flush it out.

Since the bad experience started, I had not been taking any drugs but did smoke cigarettes to help me relax. Which really did not help. So, I thought to myself: *I already have a good start, not having done any drugs for five days. Now I need to flush out my system, and I will be right as rain in a few days.* Once again, I was wrong. Everything I was experiencing was just as alive as ever. It was the most difficult thing I have ever gone through in my entire life. I was still seeing evil images, demonic shadows that seemed to follow me everywhere, and the fear of losing my mind persisted, plaguing my every thought.

Personally, looking back, I believe that at this stage, short of a miracle, it was too late. I had already been experiencing these hallucinations and thoughts for eleven days. Pure evil had a hold of my mind. But I still did not give up or lose hope I would find an answer. I needed a savior. I needed help. So far, through my own efforts I was getting nowhere. This whole time I kept visualizing a clenched fist that was telling me: *Keep fighting. Do not give up.* I did not know where this thought was coming from, but I truly believe, looking back, that it was God giving me just enough strength to get through this horrific phenomenon.

It was Saturday, sundown. Hanging out with my friends, I was attempting to skateboard at Laguna Hills High. I could not really skateboard properly when everything around me kept moving, shadows kept taunting me, and my hallucinations were barricading my every thought. I could barely keep it straight when talking to friends without giving subtle hints that there was a problem with me. I told my friends that I was going to call my mom to have her pick me up. My friends looked at me like I was crazy, a reaction I obviously did not like. They wanted to go score some drugs and hang out. Plus, it was a Saturday night, not even dark yet; the night was young. I told them I was not interested. My friends knew something was up, but I kept any details concealed.

I ended up calling my mom; she was shocked at the hour. She could pick me up, she said, but that she was going to a church function. My mom was pretty involved in a Christian church. From time to time, she even made me go. Eventually, I'd been allowed to stop attending since I would either ditch mid-church to go hang out with friends or show up extremely high from marijuana and proceed to devour the free donuts. Got to love those free donuts! Sidebar: that is also when I believe my donut addiction started. But none of my mom's devout Christian faith made sense to me. I never really paid attention in church or had any thoughts about it other than that I really disliked church. It was extremely boring and uneventful. It felt like an extension of school, and you know how I felt about school.

I ended up telling my mom that even if I had to go to the church function, to pick me up. She was shocked! This event was a farewell for a family in the congregation moving out of state. Well, I remember sitting in the back, finding it a strange experience. These church individuals were singing songs with their hands lifted high and praying to some random God. Weirded out, I ended up going to the restroom. Going to the restroom was an experience all its own. As I was about to pee, the toilet became so small it was nearly the size of a baseball; the murals from the wallpaper began coming at me, and my thoughts were consumed with fear of finally cracking and giving up on myself.

I proceeded to wander outside, sitting on a curb with my head crouched in between my legs, crying profusely. That says a lot. I used to not be a crier. My heart was so hard that I barely felt the littlest emotion.

My mom came out to ask what the problem was. I told her, "These nightmares are really getting to me." She asked to pray for me. I said, "Sure." She prayed for me, but I could barely hear her words. My mind was drifting into all the fear and doubt for my future. I did, however, tell her at that moment that maybe I could join her tomorrow morning at church. She was dumbfounded again. "Sure!" she said.

From what little sleep I got, I woke up Sunday morning hoping to find a solution at church. It was day twelve of my horror film. In church I sat with my mom in the main sanctuary, an outside venue at Laguna Hills High. The church was renting space there. As the pastor spoke, I could barely pay attention. I was so craving for him to say something that could help me. His words fell on deaf ears, barely audible over my dominant thoughts of doom. I remember listening to the pastor as he slowly disappeared, and the building behind him became what looked to be like a jail cell. I saw prison bars. I had thoughts of being trapped in my mind forever.

I left early, before the service ended, and went straight to our car, where I wept, copiously, really hard. When my mom came down to the car after the service, she saw what sort of state I was in. I felt that I was finally giving up. I'd had enough. I was going to allow whatever was going to happen next to happen. I at last told my mom the truth. I told her that I believed it was karma catching up to me. I told her of all the wrong things I'd done. I told her about all the drugs and partying. I told her the truth about the hallucinations. All the things I was seeing that I knew were not really there. All of the fears and negative thoughts that plagued my mind.

My mom wept. She was silent for a long time on the drive home. That concerned me. I was hoping she would give me instant words of comfort and wisdom. From church to home was only about a fifteen- to twenty-minute drive. I spent half the time talking about everything I'd done wrong and what I was experiencing.

We pulled into our garage, tears flooding down our faces. My mom looked at me and said something that would change my life forever. She said, "I know someone that can help you. His name is Jesus."

I remember thinking to myself: *Let's go meet Him, right now.* Hard to believe, but in the state I was in, with my mind somewhere else due to the extreme mental torment, in that instant I had no clue who this person named "Jesus" was. I thought He might be a doctor, some sort of specialist. My mother continued to say, "Jesus is God. He loves you. He cares for you. He wants to save you. But you have to commit your life 100 percent to Him. Follow Him and He will save you." At that moment, there were no questions, no hesitations or sidebar thoughts. My mother just gave me a sixty-seconds altar call to salvation.

I said unequivocally, "YES! What do we do now?" She said, "Let's pray. Repeat what I say out loud and mean it with all your heart." We prayed. I accepted Jesus Christ as my Savior, and I committed my life 100 percent to Him.

I know it sounds comical, as it is straight out of a fairy tale. Especially coming from someone like me, who has always been extremely skeptical of religion or really anything not completely explainable by tangible facts. But I can tell you, in that moment

Jesus saved me. Right after I opened my eyes from that two-minute prayer, which I said fervently, 100 percent of my hallucinations and thoughts of losing my mind were gone. I was healed in a few seconds. It was Jesus. He plucked me out of my gloomy future.

When my life had the wobbliest of foundations—with no understanding of why I existed—I aimlessly sought the approval of others. I desired to have a connection with an earthly father, who could never really fulfill me. In me, God took a person who was so unbelievably stubborn, cold-hearted, and calloused in almost every way, even at such an early age. He broke me down in order to build me up—exchange the weakest of foundations for the strongest. I believe it was probably the only path for me to know Jesus. I was that ornery. Had it not been for Jesus, I would have lost my mind. If I had not had that terrible experience, which I am so grateful for, I believe I would have lived a limited existence—probably dying unhappy and extremely unfulfilled.

I did exactly what I promised God. I committed my life 100 percent to Him. In that moment I knew I needed to clean up my act and set myself down on a new foundation, go in a new direction. Heading straight to my room with a trash can, I threw away all of my pornography, items that I stole from random stores, trashing any drugs, paraphernalia, or anything else I believed was not pleasing to God. Then I went outside to take the family dog for a walk and smoke a cigarette. I remember trying to quit smoking multiple times and failing. I lit the smoke, took a puff, and thought: *This does not please my body. Therefore, it does not please my God.* I put out the cigarette, threw away the pack, and quit for good.

God says in multiple books of the Bible that after you accept Him as your Lord and Savior, He will provide you with a helper. This helper is the Holy Spirit, who is also God. Basically, God enters you. He guides you, directs you, and blesses you! This is a beautiful thing that God provides for His people. And by His people, I mean those who accept Jesus as God for what He did for us on the cross. God is faithful in pursuing us, even when we do not pursue Him. I gave up all my old friends, as they were not the best example for me. I devoted my life to learning about God in His word, the books of the Bible. From that moment on, He took me on a wild journey, which I will share in future books.

Putting in the work, I graduated high school several months early. Now I was at a place where I was thinking about going to college, which had never been a thought before. I prayed and pondered. Crazily enough, I had multiple choices. I decided to attend a college in central California, in a little town called Hume Lake in the Sequoia National Forest. It was a boot camp–type Christian college called "Joshua Wilderness Institute." Similar to a seminary school but on steroids. One of the most amazing experiences of my life.

I got to live up in the secluded mountains for two years. The nearest town of significance is about sixty miles away; the population of Hume Lake at the time was no more than a couple hundred people. It was extremely private. It was a period I needed to get grounded in my faith and discover what I wanted to do with my life. I thoroughly enjoyed every moment. Thank God for that beautiful season.

As you can see from my story, my first life was filled with uncertainty. I had only the flimsiest of foundations—rather, didn't have one. I was coasting along day to day, not giving my future and reason for *being* much thought. Hadn't the vaguest notion of my purpose. I did learn multiple valuable lessons. And those, I am incredibly grateful for. Fortunately, my reckless choices forced me into a desperate situation. I had to decide to fight for life and figure out the meaning of all existence or to give up on life and *allow what was happening to me to simply happen*. I am firmly convinced now that Jesus had a plan for my life, and He alone gave me the strength to get through all my tough times. But at the end of the day, it was inevitably my choice. Preceded by much resistance, I chose Him.

In order for you to know your foundation, you need to know the purpose of human existence. I believe God created this playground we call Earth as a stepping stone for the life to come after we pass on from this life. What we do in this life matters to God. You either believe in God or you do not. *I am not here to convince you that what I believe is the truth.* But I do believe that God created us for a specific reason. By design we are supposed to be in relationship with God. He desires that connection with you.

These specific reasons are clearly identified in multiple ways. You can see them in a series of historical documents, in the Bible. You can see these reasons in creation. Finally, God's character and design has been inputted into each one of us. God designed us based on His own nature.

A person who does not know their foundation will have limited (insufficient) reasons for existence. A limited purpose in life. A limited passion. This person will also have limited motivation. Without purpose, passion, and motivation, it will be hard to accomplish anything.

I am here to tell you that Jesus Christ is God. He did exist here over two thousand years ago. He was crucified on a cross. He did rise from the grave three days later. He is alive and living in the lives of those who accept what He has done for us. I believe that Jesus paid the ultimate price that no one else could pay for the wrong that we have done in our life. No one is perfect. There is not one person besides Jesus who has lived a sinless life. There are consequences for the wrong we do. We do not need to suffer those consequences. There is a God who wants to save you. This God's name is "Jesus Christ." If you would only accept what He has done for you and commit your life 100 percent to Him, He will change your life for good, as He did mine nearly twenty-two years ago.

God took a lost and broken individual in me and gave me a second chance. I was losing my mind, headed for a straitjacket, but God took my shattered mind and healed me *in an instant.* This is only through the power of Jesus. He wants to bless you. He wants you to thrive in this life. He wants to give you a firm foundation that will give you the purpose, passion, and motivation to live an abundant Life. Just think of having at your fingertips the God who created all. He designed it in a way that He would be our ultimate resource.

Regardless of your circumstances, God is near you. He hears you. He loves you. He has changed billions of lives over the centuries. He is calling you to be His own. Regardless of your current lifestyle, choose Him today and forever. He is faithful to restore and heal your brokenness.

If you do not choose Christ today, *this book is still for you.* These authentic habits in the chapters that follow will allow you to dig into who you really are. Not who or what other people tell you you are but who you were designed to be. Knowing your foundation is only the beginning of this process of discovering your authentic self. Your authentic self is waiting for you.

Mission

An individual's calling in life

> First, find your purpose. Then you will
> be introduced to your passion in life.
>
> —*Anonymous*

O ur goal in this chapter is to Discover Your Life's Mission. Now, this mission can change as time goes on, but it is important for you to *know your specific calling*. Don't you find it intriguing to wonder what it is?

Certainty is something we all crave. Discovering your specific calling is Habit 2. If you do not know it, you will be living in an uncertain state. When we think of certainty, we think of confident individuals who carry themselves with a sense of pride in life. When you are certain about your calling, then beyond what you could imagine, that ignites your purpose and passion. Are you ready to stop limiting your purpose and passion for life? Are you ready to take complete ownership of your life?

Certainty allows us to have meaning, and that meaning sparks our passion to be relentless. If you want to discover your life's mission, it is going to require significant effort. You will need to ask questions like, "Why am I on this planet? What will people say about me at the end of my life? What do I want to be remembered for? What is my legacy? What do I want my legacy to be?" Hang on tight. Are you ready to get started discovering your mission and see yourself blazing with passion?

Are you one of those people who knows what they will be doing for the next six to twelve months but have no clear picture of their entire life's assignment? If you go about your life just focused on the next few months, you will find yourself putting effort into relationships, businesses, and hobbies that do not serve your life's mission. You have been given a life that is eighty to a hundred years at best. Your time is limited. Make your time on this Earth fulfilling by discovering your specific calling. Habit 2—finding your specific mission—is not for the faint of heart. If you are really serious about it, get ready to put in the work.

If you do not own a journal, now is the time to get one. It will require many journal sessions and quiet times with yourself to succeed in this habit. To identify your mission, you will need to ask yourself multiple challenging questions. This is going to be an intense journey of getting to know yourself. It will be worth the effort if you do not give up. Trust the process, be patient, and put in the work beyond just reading this chapter.

I believe that every person is uniquely designed and created as God intended. There is not one person who is the same as another. We might seem the same on the surface, but we all have a uniqueness factor. A different serial code. It makes us special. With that uniqueness, God has created us for a specific reason. A unique mission.

In order to know your mission, you must begin by asking the right questions. The right questions will give you the right answers. But going back to our individual uniqueness: there is not a set of generic questions for each person. As each person is different,

different questions will emerge. This chapter will help you facilitate the correct starting point to allow you to find your mission.

When you discover that, watch out, World, as here you'll come, ready to conquer. When someone knows their mission, whatever passion they have will rise to a completely new level. Those around you will marvel at your clarity and focus. You will be admired, as many people do not know their mission.

With clarity comes precision. That precision will allow you to accomplish much in this life. Without that precision, you will be driving in a car with foggy windows. And when you cannot see clearly, you will miss all the signposts to an abundant life. That is why knowing your mission is a crucial element in finding your authentic self.

It is a beautiful thing to know your destination before you arrive. Professional athletes, highly successful, know they will be champions before they were ever champions. They visualized the journey and the road ahead. They saw themselves as champions, so they became champions. In order for you to become a champion in the first place, you need to know your mission. Knowing your mission is the beginning of becoming a champion in life.

It personally took me many years to learn my mission. Even though I made a life-transforming decision to accept Jesus and achieved my first authentic habit (discovering my Foundation), and though I had a ton of passion for life, I was still left with no specific direction. Not knowing how to direct my life-transforming decision, I was like a boat captain in the middle of the ocean with no specific destination in mind. I had so many possible directions I could go in that I did anything and everything I could get my hands on that seemed a good way to learn something new and generally grow as a person.

I was doing positive things. Personally and professionally growing. But I still didn't really know my mission; that is, what was I designed to accomplish in life? Where was I going? What action went with knowing my mission? None surfaced. Not until decades later.

Once I discovered that, my passion went to another level. My drive was unquenchable. My certainty was through the roof. I knew where I was headed. I could see clearly. It became impossible to stop me from accomplishing that mission.

Looking back, I read plenty of self-help books to guide me to find answers during nearly two decades. I spent time nearly daily with God, reading and meditating on His words, praying for wisdom and guidance. I was always searching for my mission. I did have a clear enough lens to see the next two to three years. Even though I did not know my mission, God still directed me to accomplish beautiful things with my life. I discovered in searching for my life's mission that some things were not going to come easy. That is why, in part, I believe God created us: so that we may struggle and learn how to grow with all the many tools given us.

I graduated from college. The best career field for me, I deduced, would be entrepreneurship. I have been my own boss and business owner for eighteen years now. I met a woman with whom I fell madly in love and inevitably married her. We have been happily married fifteen years. We have two amazing kids. My son is turning five soon, and my daughter is almost seven—along with countless other ways God has blessed me. I am not short on successes and the many blessings God has bestowed on me. But oddly, this all happened without knowing my specific mission. I still felt incomplete.

I did not know how to go about detecting my mission. I was given little mission morsels here and there from elements that make up the whole but could never really unveil the full assignment. When I finally did discover my mission, did I know all the little details of my journey to come? No. But I became clear on the destination, just not the journey. The journey is the fun part, and that is the mystery of it. That is what we get to experience and learn as we go. With complete trust in God and tools to guide us along the way, it will be an abundant journey; that, I am clear on.

Sadly, I believe that some people will find their mission towards the very last season of life, even on their deathbed. People tend to coast through life and do not always put in the work to develop themselves to be their best version. They experience life as it comes. Instead of anticipating the process and knowing the outcome, they just allow life to happen. Could you imagine waiting until you're on your deathbed to realize your life's mission? Now, on the one hand, it would be great to know your mission at the end of your life, as some people do not ever discover it. But how much more blessed to know it earlier!!

I bet you would have a new level of appreciation for life. You would smell the roses in your path. You would take in all the heartache life at times has to offer and embrace the pain. Pain means you are alive! You would live in the moment, knowing that whether your circumstances were good or bad, you would fight another day. It is that awareness that allows you to go to a new level. Knowing your specific mission in life will get you one step closer to finding your authentic self.

Think of it this way: can you remember an instance where you had a task to accomplish but lacked all clues as to where to begin or how you were going to arrive? In most cases, you probably just figured it all out as you went along. The only problem with this strategy is that you will find yourself aimlessly moving in either the right direction or the wrong direction. And once the task is completed, it might not be up to your standards or your overall desired outcome.

As stated in the previous chapter, I discovered my Foundation on July 15, 2001. It was not until summertime of 2019 that I started the process to discover my Mission. I was thirty-six years old. I had spent approximately eighteen years in the dark about it. Not knowing that calling was unbelievably frustrating. I had to be on Earth for some purpose, but what? I always admire those who have their specific calling figured out.

Mentally, I was now in a place where I was going to do something about it. It is important to say I was very happy and content. But I have always been one to push the envelope on working on myself since God changed my life. I was always looking to develop my relationship with God and to develop my relationship with myself, knowing who I really am as a person, one called a child of God.

At the time, in journaling, I ramped up the questions I was asking myself: tough questions. But I barely touched on the real one. Questions like "Where do I see myself in thirty years? Fifty years?" All the way to the ripe age of one hundred? True fact, I have always seen myself living to at least one hundred. We shall see what God thinks about that. Will He allow it to happen?

So, in early 2019, I was wrestling with these questions but not going deep enough. I was doing what an intentional person would do on a first date with someone they'd just met. I asked all the basic questions. Plus, I dove deep and asked the tough questions. My wife and I, for example, got most of the tough questions out of the way on our first date. We have been together for eighteen years now. There is something to learn from asking hard questions to others and, most importantly, yourself. That's how you gain new perspective and attain the next level of growth.

I have always been one to dig deep with other people. It was time for me to dive deep with myself—*on another level*. In that season I challenged how I went about doing things—what my thought processes were.

Finally, after a few months of putting in the work—journaling, praying, and meditating—I discovered my mission. It hit me like a ton of bricks. It was November 2019. I went for a short, eight-mile run on a frosty, gloomy day. I was prepping for an ultramarathon I had signed up to run in January 2020 on Catalina Island.

An ultramarathon is a traditional marathon (26.2 miles) on steroids. The first ultramarathon distance normally starts at 50 kilometers (31 miles). I was going to run a 50-mile ultramarathon on

Catalina Island. It is an amazing race that has roughly eight thousand feet of elevation to climb, over all sorts of terrain. If you like to run, I highly recommend that race.

Most people either like to run or they hate it. I like to run, but I also understand how tough it is on the body. I typically run in moderation. For the runners out there, you understand what it is like to go for a nice run and get that runner's high. That is exactly what I experienced in November. Typically when I run, I get that infamous runner's high. My mind thinks crystal clearly, and I am able to process my thoughts at a quicker rate.

During this run—right in the midst of it, "in the zone,"—I began thinking about creating a new business. That took me down my normal rabbit hole of putting together a "road map" of what it would look like, from A to Z. By "road map" I mean business plan. Fact—the term "road map" was first coined by Tony Robbins, several of whose week-long workshops I've attended. I consider him a mentor and great teacher to me. He is truly an example of someone living an authentic life. Thank you, Tony, for your passion and zeal to help others. You are an inspiration for all to see!

Obviously, I was in the middle of a run, so the road map I came up with was rudimentary, a rough draft. But paramount in starting a business is having a company's mission statement. It tells you where the company is going.

As I was thinking of a business mission statement for this company—still running, my legs rhythmically encouraging my thoughts to flow—I randomly thought: *What is my personal mission statement? I know it for business. What about for me personally?* Now, obviously I had been working assiduously at trying to discover my mission for several months, but I had not thought about it like a business. My brain works quite systematically. If I weren't an entrepreneur, I would probably be an engineer. I typically have a hard time skipping steps when I know in most cases one thing needs to precede another. For instance, if you are going to recite the alphabet, you would start with the letter A and go all the way through Z. You wouldn't skip.

What I realized was that when thinking about what my mission was, I was not following my own system of A through Z. I was trying to skip steps. In creating a business, you start with the foundation, *as we did with our first authentic habit.* From there, you ask the right questions to nail down the purpose of the business and what it needs if to sustain growth.

I simply was not asking myself the right questions. It was not until I started to ask myself these new questions I'd never addressed before that I found the answer. I realized it was right in front of my face the whole time. I needed to start with the right questions.

Questions like: *"Where do I want to be at the end of my life? What accomplishments do I want to achieve?"* I had already posed these questions to myself, but too casually. I needed to probe more— and in the right sequence. Envisioning how I would get to where I wanted to be at the end of my life, I tried to uncover more about myself. *Don't flinch,* I told myself. *What am I good at? What are my talents? What sort of things come naturally to me? How can I profit not financially but spiritually and emotionally from my mission? Selfishly, what do I want to do with my life? Who do I want to be? How can I become the superhero of my story?"* Suddenly, in that runner's high, in an instant of peak understanding, all the answers came rushing through my head—telling me my mission in limpid clarity.

It was amazing. So simple. Right in front of my face. How had I not seen it? My mission is "To Build a Legacy of Faith in Christ, Love for other People, & the Freedom Found in Enterprise."

That's it. For me, I do not care to build earthly wealth that will not go with me when I die and go on to my real, eternal home. One of the most important things for me is to instill the truth of Christ and His sacrifice for us into my children. Fundamentally, my legacy is to my children. I would do anything for them. Parents understand that love.

The shortened version of my mission is "To Build a Legacy of Faith, Love, and Entrepreneurship."

In uncovering my mission, of all the questions above, I discovered that to me the final one—that shot all the answers into an alignment—a synthesis, was, "What words would I use to describe what I am passionate about?" Easy. I knew that right off: "Legacy, Faith, Love, and Entrepreneurship." Not a pause or moment's hesitation.

Once I came up with the words that impacted my soul, then my mission glowed to me, in its clarity. Certainty pumped through my body. I became unstoppable.

From then on, if something did not fall in line with that mission? It was not worth my time. Time is precious. We all know that. The limited amount I have, I want to spend wisely. The younger Jake would do anything and everything to grow as an individual. Even if not in the best interests of my long-term goals, I would do it in order just to learn something new. I realized how much time I'd wasted. That lesson took a long time to sink in.

I am a man on a mission. Now I know my mission in life. *I do not know the journey*, but I do know the destination. If you want to master this second authentic habit—of discovering your mission—I recommend you *practice three activities: Journal, Pray, and Meditate.* One: buy a journal and start regularly writing your thoughts down. Two: pray aloud. This will help you process your thoughts. Three: meditate on a single thought. Let me take the time to break each one of these down.

Go out and buy a journal—not necessarily fancy or expensive. Something that will allow you to get your thoughts out on paper. My director, Darin McWatters, in college always said, "It is one thing to think a thought, but it is a whole other ballpark to be able to write out in clear, precise words what you are thinking." If you want to discover your mission, this needs to be a daily activity, I believe. Of course, there are going to be some days you skip.

Don't assume you need to put in an abnormal amount of time. At the very least, five minutes a day. Do it at the time of day when your mind is clearest. For me, it is the first thing in the morning. For you, it could be in the middle of the day, in between work or your normal daily routines. Or, before bed. Everyone does it differently and at different times, but the point is, you do it regularly, if not daily.

As you have probably observed, I like structure. I like to follow structured guidelines when doing my journaling. Every few months I change up that structure. For instance, I will tell myself I am going to journal about three items a day: thanks to God, personal goals, and prayers to God. That structure might not be the right fit for you. The whole premise behind getting a journal is to get to know yourself. You will need to start asking the right questions. Getting all of your thoughts out onto paper will allow you to think more clearly. Putting your mind on paper will give you something tangible to show yourself you're moving in the right direction.

Do not put a ton of pressure on yourself. It is not always necessary to fill out an entire page or even a large paragraph. It could be as simple as a few sentences. In order to find success journaling, simplify the process by taking the pressure off your shoulders. Let yourself perform less. Write down good questions and really sit in your thoughts. Try to write the best possible answers. Sometimes it is difficult to get past all the layers of lies we have embedded inside ourselves.

Try to find out the real answers. Your real answers. They are different for each person. God has made us all uniquely different. We all have different desires. We all have different wants. We all have different journeys we live. At the end of the day, put in the time journaling, and you will reap the rewards of knowing yourself better. Really get to know yourself. Become best friends with yourself. In turn, you will eventually discover your authentic mission. Not the mission that other people have for you. It is your choice to decide who you want to be. You always have a choice. God has blessed everyone with the gift of choice.

Prayer allows you to process your thoughts. Especially, praying aloud solidifies your thoughts. Now, maybe you have not decided to have a personal relationship with Jesus Christ. Even if you do not believe in God at all, this practice will still benefit you. Just like journaling allows you to get your thoughts out on paper, praying aloud allows you to articulate your emotions. Praying gives you the opportunity to discover your authentic mission. The positive emotion that comes from praying will get you in the right state of mind. It will allow you to progress in the right direction, one step closer.

Think of skilled comedians. They not only write their own jokes but also practice audibly delivering those jokes to an audience. We all know people who have good jokes but can't deliver them. Those people are not very funny, even if they have the best jokes or stories. Some people do not have the best jokes but know how to deliver jokes with the right words, timing, and tone, which makes them extremely funny. All that to say, there is power in audibly speaking your thoughts aloud.

If you do have a personal relationship with God, then praying will be even more impactful for you. Praying allows you to dialogue with the one true God of the universe, Your Savior and best friend. To share all your emotions, thoughts, fears, failures, and anything else that you want to talk about with Him. Praying is so vital to maintaining a healthy, positive relationship with God.

God loves you. God wants to hear from you, even if He knows what you are about to say. He wants to hear it from your mouth. Praying is an essential method for developing your personal relationship with God. It is no different than the relationships in your life with people you love. These people you love, I bet you regularly talk to them, ask them questions, pursue them through meaningful conversations.

If you have never prayed a day in your life and do not know where to begin, that is completely fine—it's not too late to begin. Start by finding a quiet place where you can think without distraction.

Let me provide you with a simple format for praying successfully. Remember these three topics: Thanks, Desires, and Strengths. Begin your prayer announcing all of your thanks in life. You might or might not focus these thanks on something specific. Next, declare aloud (or silently) all of the personal desires or wants you have for other people and yourself. Finally, request strength for others to accomplish their dreams and goals in life. And you likewise to accomplish yours.

That prayer format is as simple as it gets. Do not overthink it. Just audibly put in the work to vocalize what is on your mind and heart. It will get you one step closer to fully understanding your calling in life. Knowing that calling is crucial to discovering your authentic self, digging deep, moving past all the layers of lies you have been told—that you are not good enough, you are not capable, you need to be or act a certain way because that is what is expected of you.

Finally, you can meditate in many different ways. Learn how to focus on a single thought. Start with one thought that you have not fully developed, something that maybe you wrestle with understanding. The process of knowing yourself and fully understanding your mission is not for those who just want to coast in life. It will require a strong work ethic and a ton of personal fortitude.

Meditating is the last of the three daily activities that will help you discover your mission. Journaling starts the process by getting your thoughts on paper. Praying further gets your thoughts into words, which moves you into mental and physical action. Meditating allows you to fully understand those thoughts. People are intimidated by the idea of meditating. I believe it is because we typically have a hard time resting in our own thoughts. Sometimes the most difficult person to face is yourself.

One of your greatest assets in life is to know yourself. Spending time meditating gives you the breathing room to know yourself deeper and on a new level. As I stated, meditating can be done in many different fashions. I would recommend finding a place of peace for yourself—somewhere at home, on a hike, during a run, at the beach, or even up in the mountains. Everyone has a different place of peace. Discover your place; then be still and "know thyself." Be still and know that God is near. Be still and know you are never alone, as God is right by your side.

During meditation, clear your mind. Focus on only one thought. Whatever your thought, develop it into understanding and fully learn what it means. Put in the time. Thoughts related to unfinished business often run through our head. We have ideas not fully processed, and goals that we did not realize whether they meant little or a lot to us. We pondered concepts that made no sense but got us excited about something new and different.

Meditating is simply taking the time to understand. The beginning of understanding is knowing yourself. Knowing yourself is the beginning of knowing your calling. Knowing your calling is to understand your mission. Once you understand your mission, you will be ready for the next habit, Habit 3—to make a strategical blueprint sketching out just how you will implement the steps to proceed to, in the end, knowing your authentic self.

Be relentless in your daily practice of journaling, praying, and meditating. Do not give up on yourself. You will discover your true mission if you believe you will. Though it will require work and a ton of personal effort, it will be worth it. Think of the new level of purpose and passion you will discover in yourself. The drive that will be unquenchable.

No one can stop you but yourself. Pursue your purpose and passion by understanding what your authentic mission is in this life. There is no time like the present. *Carpe* NOW! The Latin phrase carpe diem means "seize the day." I like to say *carpe* now: seize the moment! Seize this very moment to become your best version. To discover your authentic self by discovering your specific mission in life. Now is the time to get to work. See your future self beckoning.

Blueprint

Framework for realizing success

> Make at least one definite move
> daily toward your goals.
>
> —*Bruce Lee*

As far back as I can remember, I have always loved to create. Specifically, I love creating systems. What a great feeling, to create something tangible and real when it comes from nothing. Just a simple concept in your mind that became reality. I also love being free from obligation to do something I do *not* believe in. For that reason, I'm an entrepreneur. I love building things from nothing and having the freedom to do it as I please. I also love the risk and adrenaline behind laying it all on the line. Creating businesses is never the same experience twice, or three times, or four, as has happened to me. Each company I created and built has been a journey. There is always something new and exciting on the horizon.

For the last eighteen years, I built businesses—started twelve companies. Now, these were not big, but small businesses. It gave me an appreciation for hard work and persistent diligence to get the job done with excellence in mind. In the last two decades of business, I have had more failures than successes.

About 80 percent of my companies, I would consider to be a failure. I would also consider that with those failures I learned tons of valuable lessons I carried with me to the next company. The other 20 percent were golden, absolutely a win. The companies that succeeded had just the right key ingredients for a great company: they changed lives in the surrounding community and made money in the process. Those two key elements have always gone hand in hand for me. I do not want to make money without changing lives. I cannot change lives unless I make money. Those two key points are vital for any company I create or am a part of.

Creating systems for companies is a passion of mine. To put together a plan—a roadmap—for success and growth, I find eminently rewarding. It takes a lot of *self*-growth to grow a company. After you conceive an idea, immediately you need to put together a system that will serve as the backbone for your company. This system is most commonly called a business plan. I have always thought of it as a blueprint, or game plan.

Now, once created, this blueprint can change as unforeseen obstacles are thrown your way, but there always needs to be a blueprint. Currently, I am in one of the more difficult businesses to be in right now. I am the broker and owner of Barrena Real Estate Group, which primarily focuses on residential real-estate sales in South Orange County, California.

All around us, other real-estate offices and agents have saturated that county. We are experiencing higher interest rates, which in turn prevents a large portion of homeowners from putting their home on the market. That has made our housing inventory historically low. Due to the higher interest rates, we have fewer buyers looking for homes. The remaining home buyers are having a tough time finding a home since inventory is low. Currently, the buyers outnumber the homes, so it is quite competitive for the homes that are left. It is not an easy time to buy a home when there are not a lot of homes on the market.

All that said, it only poses a temporary problem. Change the blueprint—change the outcome. A large number of real-estate brokers and agents are jumping ship. As I said, it is tough right now. Personally, to jump ship is not in my DNA. I do not give up on what I believe in. Before the real-estate industry shifted, I had a blueprint all planned out. Now I've had to make multiple adjustments to tailor it to our changed housing climate. That is the fun part of being a business owner, being able to respond agilely when circumstances require. I've learned to always expect new obstacles on the horizon.

To properly strategize growth, having a company blueprint is paramount. Without a solid framework in place, there is no organization. If there is no organization, that company is doomed to fail. I am sure there are companies out there that have had success with a poor blueprint, or business plan. But more times than not, it is absolutely necessary to have a solid game plan to accomplish a company's mission and goals.

I am in the real-estate industry, but it is not the real estate that drives me. It is not the profits alone, but also the job of being able to help our community. Not everyone is rolling in the South OC money. Some people have genuine hardships, financial or circumstantial. I value being able to come in with my team and offer assistance to our clients. I would not be able to offer consistent help without my team. I am so thankful for all the individuals working with me. We are a new company but growing, as our team now consists of over twenty. I do not care to have a large team, only the right team. The right individuals— aligned with my company's blueprint—who want to truly impact lives in our community. And make some money in the process.

As a business owner, I would not know what type of team members I was looking for had I not initially created a company blueprint. I have created companies in the past where many facets were working correctly, but other areas were missing the necessary elements for overall success. I did not realize it at the time, but I was missing fundamental blueprint elements.

Maybe you are not a business owner—have no desire to be one. Maybe you are an athlete. Well, I have been competitive in almost every sport I've played. I was not big into team sports, growing up, and in my adult years. I gravitated towards skateboarding, as you know, but also snowboarding, mixed martial arts, and golfing. I was so competitive that even though I did not really pick up a golf club until my mid-twenties, within a short couple of years I competed professionally. I even went to Q-School, a term used in professional golf to represent annual tournaments that *qualify* a golfer to make it onto one of the world's leading golf tours: for example, the PGA, LPGA, and European Tours. I did not end up making it on the PGA (Professional Golfers Association of America) Tour. Nor did I get very far in my golf career, but I did get extremely good at a game that requires a lot of meticulous detail.

I say all this not to toot my own horn but to illustrate that in order for me to succeed at these sports, I had to put in the work. And before that, I put together a blueprint: a simple game plan to get me to focus on the right things to improve in the areas I wanted to. For example, golf in my mind was broken down into four areas of improvement—four skills: short game, long game, putting, and mental game. I broke down each category, evaluating my weaknesses and strengths in each. I would not put as much effort into my strengths. However, my weaknesses I would try to improve on inch by inch, day by day. It was a tedious process, but I got really good.

In the long run, I did not get as good as I needed to compete at the highest level. But it taught me a lot about business and life. You see, when people attempt to compete at the highest level in sports or business, they put together a plan of attack. This plan of attack is what I am calling the blueprint. Think of it as your framework for success. In order to grow as an athlete or in business, it is necessary for you to strategize. If you do not have a detailed plan, you will most likely not get very far. Therefore, your blueprint of attack is of utmost importance if you want to apply these authentic habits in this book to your life.

Question—How many people do you know put together a blueprint, or business plan, for their own life? A game plan for their own personal growth? In my experience, I have not seen many. I have realized over the decades that this is a missing element with people who are trying to create authentic habits. They might focus on establishing a new habit of fitness, for example, yet they do not really have a clear picture of what that looks like practically. Or how to apply fitness to their life. They focus on habits without focusing on the system or framework of putting them all together in a cohesive manner.

In this book, we are looking at *ten habits—Foundation, Mission, Blueprint, Perseverance, Fitness, Community, Selflessness, Growth, Discipline, and Mindset–to create your authentic self.* Even before mastering the rest of these habits *in the chapters ahead*, you need to know, *at the outset*, how you intend to *implement* all ten—that is, how to put them all together in a system that works for your specific life, in your lifestyle. I call this making a blueprint.

I do not want to see you fail. I only want to see you succeed. You cannot succeed except with the *right blueprint*—a launching pad to get you to do the right things in a manner that works for you. Your blueprint will not be flawless. It will be ever-changing, as your life is constantly changing. If you meet with resistance and are struggling to stick to these new habits, then you will need to make a change in your blueprint. That's completely normal. You will do that the rest of your life.

I am extremely excited about sharing my blueprint strategy, as this could literally change your life. And I am in the business of changing lives. It is a template blueprint that I use for my own life. It has served me well over the years and is highly effective if done properly. I will be breaking down each step into enough detail to guide you into writing a completed blueprint of your own.

I would highly recommend getting something to take notes with and start right now the process of creating your blueprint. As we go through each step below, take the time to create your own steps. Remember, this is a discovery process that requires your effort. The end game goal is to know your authentic self. Creating your personal blueprint is absolutely necessary at the outset. Here we go!

Step 1) Foundation—Purpose of Existence, in General

In Chapter 1, I spoke in detail about the importance of laying the proper foundation. That Foundation is your *first Habit and starting point at each turn in the road*. Here too. Not surprisingly, in order to create your authenticity blueprint, you need to start, again, with the very same Foundation, that is, with Habit 1. In this case, it will be a variation on or restatement of Habit 1.

Mine is completely personal. Yours can be entirely different, but I use mine to illustrate. It goes like this: "Jesus Christ is the one true God. He is my number one in this life. He is my personal Savior and best friend." My one true, firm foundation. I believe He is that for all people, but that's my opinion. If I did not share that truth with you, I would not be authentic to who I am. God has given me a heart to love people. I am not the best at loving people all the time. I make mistakes often. I know God has a heart for people that is far greater than mine. He wants the utmost best for us all.

I am not writing all this to force you to make a decision or make you feel uncomfortable. If you do not believe, that's your choice. I accept that, but I know God is relentless. He remains diligent to win your heart! He does want to have a personal relationship with you. He wants to change your life for the better. He wants to bless you for all of eternity if you would just acknowledge Him for what he has done by paying the ultimate price for all our mistakes.

It is important that whatever you decide is your foundation, it must be your everything. Start your blueprint based on *a foundation that shakes you to your core*. Now let's go to *the next step in building your life's blueprint*.

Step 2) Mission—Your Calling

Remember, finding your specific mission is as simple as becoming best friends with yourself. Get to know yourself on a deeper level.

As I stated in the previous chapter, in Habit 2, you need to put in the work to discover that mission. If you have not put in the work, there is no time like the present: start journaling on a daily basis; write down all of your thoughts. This will help crystallize what is festering deep down in your cerebellum. Then, vocalize aloud those thoughts in a prayer. Even if you do not believe in God, it will help you process those thoughts. If you believe in God, it will allow you to draw near Him and also process those thoughts on a deeper level. Finally, spend time meditating on a single thought. Really understand that thought. Try to dig in deep inside yourself and answer the questions that frustrate you most. Answering those questions will allow you to discover a new side of yourself.

Once you know that mission, you will be on fire for life. You will be driven by purpose and passion that is noticeable to all who see you. Here is my full and short mission:

Full Mission: To Build a Legacy of Faith in Christ, Love for other People & the Freedom Found in Enterprise.

Short Mission: To Build a Legacy of Faith, Love & Entrepreneurship.

The important thing is, put in the work to discover yourself. Through that self-discovery you will know your specific mission and be ready to create your next blueprint step.

Step 3) Slogan—Mission Motivator

Think of a slogan that is an abbreviated version of your mission. Now, I have seen a decent portion of people create missions for their life, but how many have a slogan in life? This was something I found to be a missing link in the lives of those seeking to accomplish their mission. I stumbled upon creating a blueprint for my life through thinking about all of the business plans I've created over the years. It was through that self-discovery I realized that I'd created multiple business plans over the years, but I was not doing it for myself.

I say all that because most businesses have a slogan. So why shouldn't a person have a slogan? I came up with my slogan nearly a decade ago for myself: "Carpe NOW." More on this in a later chapter in this book.

But I will say, my slogan motivates me to seize the day right NOW. It reminds me to stay on course. When thinking of your slogan, allow it to be short and sweet. The words must be impactful to you.

Step 4) Vision—Short- & Long-Term Goals

This one is always extremely exciting to me.

My recommendation is to reverse-engineer your goals. Start with the very end of your life. Visualize every little detail. Visualize exactly who you want to be and what you will look like at every stage of your life. Ask yourself hard questions. Where do you want to be in one year, five years, ten, twenty-five, fifty, and beyond? We are all at different seasons in our life and have different circumstances. Use your foundation, mission, and slogan as a starting point to cultivate your goals.

Remember, your goals will serve your mission. If your goals are not helping you reach your life's mission, they are not worth your time. The only person who is going to set you up for success in reaching your goals is yourself. Screw your head on straight, know who you are, put in the work to visualize, write them down, and realize your life's goals!

Step 5) Service—Mission Field

Regardless of your mission, you have a mission *field*. We all do! In this step it is important to know exactly who or what that is. If it is a specific region or group or entity or whatever else, learn about that mission field and how to serve it. Go to school on your mission field. Prepare yourself for every possible circumstance. Plan out your strategy for success. Execution will be your key ingredient to success. But if you do not know your mission field in detail, you will not be able to execute.

Step 6) Support System

Life is tough enough with people in our corner; do not go at it alone.

This step is so important it's a whole habit, with its own chapter, up ahead.

Who is in your corner? Who has your back?

Know who these people are. Identify these people and stay connected with them. It is easier to disconnect than to connect with people. It requires diligent effort to have close relationships. Put the right people in your community. If you do, you will reap the rewards of having a fulfilling, abundant life.

Step 7) Marketing—Building the Mission

In this step you will put together a simple, precise marketing plan. Yes, I said a marketing plan for your mission. Why not? Even if your mission is to be an outstanding parent, you will need to market that to your children.

Unless your mission is to be locked in a room for the rest of your life, there is always an audience for your mission.

Think of clever ways to promote your mission to your audience. Keep track of those ways. In the business world, a company will have

KPIs (key performance indicators) to track a company's performance. That is exactly what you will do with your mission. Find ways to track your success in reaching your goals.

For example, my mission is "To Build a Legacy of Faith in Christ, Love for Other People, & the Freedom Found in Enterprise." My first and foremost mission, field or audience, is my children, as they are who I want to build my legacy in. Second, everyone who would let me tell them about the love of Jesus and the salvation He provides. Third, any people in need of a helping hand. Fourth and finally, people who need to hear and learn about the benefits of being an entrepreneur and the freedom that provides.

I have created a "marketing plan" to put myself in front of my audience to accomplish that mission. Here is a part of it. Building my legacy in my kids: I have two children that I regularly spend time with, separately and together. I not only regularly date my wifey, but I date my kiddos. My goal is to have the right relationship balance of friendship, fathering and mentoring with my kids. This will allow me to instill my legacy into my children. I offer up one of the most valuable things we all have: time, knowledge, and expertise.

See, it does not take much. The idea is that you are aware it will take a deliberate and specific plan to accomplish your mission in life. Focus on your marketing plan so that you will accomplish your mission.

Step 8) Income—Financial Life Support

How will you support your life? How will you support those around you?

No need to go on about this one, as there are countless books, podcasts, and information available on how to make money. Money is the primary focus of most individuals in the world. To a decent portion of people, financial success is everything. I believe building financial wealth is important but only a small piece of the puzzle to helping an individual live a fulfilling and purpose-filled life.

Discover how you want to finance your mission. It does not have to be one thing for the rest of your life. That is the beauty of having an entrepreneur's mindset. Answer these two questions:

- ONE: *What am I most passionate about?*

  Finding something you are incredibly passionate about is key to sustainability in a career. Discover something that does not drain you but fills you up. I have been an entrepreneur for the last eighteen years, and I feel like I have not worked in two decades. It is pinch worthy. I feel like I am living a dream life. I am so grateful for that feeling.

- TWO: *How much money do I need to make to support my mission?*

  This is a crucial question that must be answered in order for you to reach your financial goals.

Answer those two questions, and you will discover your financial life support. Take the time to really think about this one, as you will be doing this most likely the rest of your life. Spend some time journaling, praying, and meditating to help you find the answers you seek. It is in the quiet places of your mind that you can discover where your heart is leading you.

Step 9) SWOT—Strengths, Weaknesses, Opportunities, & Threats

This step is crucial in putting together a proper blueprint. SWOT stands for Strengths, Weaknesses, Opportunities, & Threats. It is a normal component for most business plans. Yet it is highly effective for personal growth. I have not seen anyone apply this to themselves, which I find to be funny. I know a ton of people who are titans in the business world or other areas. But in most other important areas of their life, they are missing the mark by far.

SWOT will allow you to evaluate yourself at close quarters. First, list all of your personal strengths, then list all of your personal weaknesses. Be honest with yourself.

List all of the opportunities you can accomplish using your strengths. Think to yourself: *If I have the <u>fill in the blank</u> strength, what is my opportunity with that strength?*

Next, list every realistic threat that can happen if you fall into your weaknesses. In my opinion, it is best to focus on your strengths and not worry too much about your weaknesses. Yes, you could improve your weakness, but why when you have so many other strengths?

For example, if you own a business and you really need to fill that weakness to be a strength, hire someone who has that strength. They will do a much better job than you. Now, that is a good return on investment. To some extent, I do not see myself with many weaknesses, but strengths. Of course, I am kidding myself! Here is a case in point: I mentioned that my mind works like an engineer. I tend to overanalyze. That is a weakness. I tend to read behind the lines and go past the surface. That is not always a good thing. Sometimes, you need quick and simple reactions that I just do not possess at times. When you overanalyze as a weakness, your threat would be never making a move in the first place. Or moving too slowly, not executing in a timely manner.

Through recognizing and evaluating your SWOT, you will gain a clearer picture of what direction you should go in. Remember, your blueprint is all for the purpose of *applying a practical life plan to find—and then become—your authentic self*, one that allows you to accomplish your mission, be successful, and thrive.

Step 10) Implementation

Once you have all previous steps to your blueprint figured out, it is finally necessary to implement it into your life. This is by far the most important step, where a lot of people miss the mark.

Practically apply your blueprint by integrating it into your calendar. Whether your calendar is physical in nature or, as with most people, digital on your personal device, litter it throughout with reminders of your blueprint—making sure you keep the task at hand front and center. Use daily, weekly, monthly, quarterly, or even yearly reminders to help you stay on course. These reminders are simple calendar invites to yourself to perform a task at a given time. It is really that simple.

You will not accomplish your mission by chance. It is too easy to slip into the abyss of complacency. Be excited about your blueprint! Know that with the right strategies you will accomplish your mission. This will allow you to be one step closer to finding your authentic self. Your authentic self is waiting for you to step into who you really are, who God designed you to be: perfectly created, yet broken in nature, but authentically and perfectly you.

Perseverance

Endurance that lasts a lifetime

> Consider it all joy when you encounter various trials, knowing that the testing of your faith produces perseverance. And let perseverance have its perfect result, so that you may be perfect and complete, lacking in nothing.
>
> —*The Apostle James*

I have spent the last twenty-two years religiously working out, eating healthy food, and investing in my overall well-being. I do not just mean from a physical standpoint. I am talking from a general self-development standpoint. Believe it or not, some have told me that it is a selfish act to focus on yourself. But others state the opposite: a life of discipline and self-sacrifice, doing what is best for my overall progress in life. I have heard these comments too many times to count. Over the years it has really got me thinking about the act of self-care and self-development.

To some people, the act of investing in your health and overall vitality is self-centered. Of course, there are always examples of individuals who are excessive when it comes to investing in themselves. Let us call them extremists. They are either all in or all out. But I have observed that typically most people who invest in themselves live a more productive and fulfilling life. Yet, there are always naysayers who believe we self-developers are prioritizing the wrong things in our lives.

Some people believe that while we focus on ourselves, others get pushed to the side, allocated to second place. The funny thing is, I absolutely agree. I believe you cannot effectively help other people unless you take care of yourself first. By investing the time into your overall well-being—your physical, spiritual, mental, and professional self—you are only better equipping yourself to be successful in transforming your life and the lives around you. The more you sharpen yourself, the more effective you will be at helping those around you.

One of my go-to workouts is that I like to run. I try to run in moderation, knowing that it is rough on my body—rough on the human body in general. I still run because I enjoy the exhilaration I get in a good running cadence. It puts me in the proper headspace to think crystal clearly, in that "runner's high." I have run dozens of marathons. That extreme exertion is not for everyone but only those who like to push the limits of their body and mind. Which is my cup of tea!

In order to successfully run a marathon, you must have consistent discipline and effort. Daily. You must spend time running, rehabilitating, and planning. Most people cannot just run 26.2 miles without a proper strategy in place. Super humans don't count. Some people think running a marathon is a bit excessive, or even borderline selfish, considering that it takes multiple hours a week away from other endeavors you could indulge in doing besides focusing on running a successful marathon.

As mentioned in Chapter 1, after years of completing dozens of marathons, in 2019, I decided it was time to run my first ultramarathon. I went straight to a 50-mile race option. Not to mention, it was not the easiest ultramarathon to start with, as it was far from flat but on mountainous terrain. To be fair, most ultramarathons cover a lot of distance because they do go through the backcountry quite often.

I decided to run the January 2020 California Catalina Island ultramarathon: 50 miles with eight thousand feet of elevation gain. This was the first time in a long time that I was excited to run a race. For me, marathons had gotten a little boring. I was excited to put together a strategic blueprint of my overall running game plan. I created the training program: a solid program that would extend for five months prior to the race. It included short-, mid-, and long-range runs. Also, I put together a solid nutrition program, along with a rehabilitation program for all the damage I was going to do to my body.

Most extreme athletes make this mistake when putting together an intense training program. They typically embrace the tough workouts and proper nutrition it takes to perform, but they forget the part where it breaks down your muscles. This in turn will lead you down the path of injury: a deal breaker for all athletes. Proper routines to store your muscle function and optimal alignment is absolutely necessary. Also, even though I had marathon experience, I have always believed it is important to learn from those who have done whatever you are about to attempt for the first time. So to put together the right strategy for me, I read a few books and did my research.

Particularly helpful was *Can't Hurt Me: Master Your Mind and Defy the Odds* by retired US Navy SEAL David Goggins, himself an ultramarathon runner, ultra-distance cyclist, triathlete, public speaker, and author of his two memoirs, who was inducted into the International Sports Hall of Fame for his achievements in sports. I read it right when it came out, in December 2018. Fantastic book! More important than the techniques needed to prepare for my ultramarathon was getting into the right mindset, which I've always been a big proponent of. David hits this point harder than I've ever seen anyone else do. He brings tons of value, using his past experiences, along with practical tools, to help people push past extreme situations like running 50 miles straight. Thank you, David, for an outstanding book and an even better example you have set to build your legacy.

Let us just say, I did everything right in my preparation minus one thing: I neglected to think about the boat ride out to the island. Big mistake. *I get motion sickness.* I would not say it is a severe issue, but on a scale of 1 to 10, it is probably a 6—especially on a boat ride that would last about an hour and a half in excessively choppy waters. So around mid-morning the day before the race, I innocently took a boat ride out of San Clemente, California, to Catalina Island. But it wasn't my only mistake. As all the locals know, there are two ways to take a boat ride out to Catalina Island (unless, of course, you own your own boat or have other means).

One option is out of San Clemente; the other leaves from Long Beach. Because of the angle the boat glides over the water, it's always better to opt for Long Beach; San Clemente is known for being a long, choppy trip, whereas if you leave out of Long Beach, it is not nearly as choppy and it is roughly a forty-five-minute boat ride—a lot better than an hour and a half. Also, it is always better to leave on the first boat ride of the day, as timing affects the choppiness of the water, which is a lot smoother at that time of day. Point taken. But did I heed it? Of course not. And to make matters worse, I was aware of the two scenarios. However, since I do not severely struggle with motion sickness *every time*, I obliviously thought I could get away with it. Absolutely made a mistake on this one.

As you can imagine, my wife knows about my motion sickness. She has seen me get sick enough to know exactly when it is about to happen. We boarded the boat with our kids. She even tried to find the best place on the boat to prevent me from getting sick. Only about five minutes into our journey, I looked at my wife and she got the signal. Time for Daddy to check out for a little bit, as I was about to get pretty sick for the next TWELVE hours. I proceeded to throw up profusely in the restroom. I spent quality time with that toilet. The toilet and I became such good friends that we embraced all the way through my journey. Not literally, but you get what I'm saying.

We finally arrived on the island, with me close to helpless: I could hardly see straight. Not able to assist my wife and kids, I had to stop multiple times to throw up as everyone passed me by, feeling sorry for my situation. I really did not care about all my viewers. I just wanted to feel better as soon as possible. As bad as I felt, my mind went to my 2:00 a.m. early-morning wake-up call for the race. As you know by now, I am the type of person who plans out almost everything in life. So in order to do all my morning routine successfully before the 5:00 a.m. race time, I had to get up before the crack of dawn.

We checked into the hotel. The kids were extremely excited, bouncing all over the place. At this point, both my kids were walkers and loved to go off on their own. As parents, it requires a lot of attention on our part. And, unfortunately, Daddy was nearly tapped out. My wife was tired from the extra work of doing almost everything—including manage two rumbunctious kids—nearly by herself. After we got in our room, we realized that it was smaller than anticipated—not more than a couple hundred square feet—with my wife, two-year-old son, and four-year-old daughter squeezing in. It seemed like everything was falling apart, but I remained positive. I told myself that I would eventually get better. My plan was to get rehydrated—since I'd thrown up twenty-plus times to the point I was dry heaving—and get some food in my system.

It was right around noon when we arrived. By the time we got a cab, checked into our hotel, and made our way back down to town for dinner, it was right around 4:00 p.m. I was still feeling lousy and nauseated but able to eat. After getting what food I could take down into my system, I started to feel a little better hour by hour. We tried to get to bed at a good time, which was difficult with two little ones. My son, a restless sleeper at that point, woke up multiple times every night. We ended up getting to bed at around 9:00 p.m. That night my son woke up crying multiple times and in turn woke my daughter every time. That was probably another mistake. I love my family more than anything, but it was just making my race preparation incredibly challenging. We should have booked separate rooms.

At 2:00 a.m., I woke, feeling excited but a little woozy and dehydrated. I went through my morning routine, fired up to give the race my 100 percent best effort. I ended up making it to the starting line well in time to get ready for the race to start at 5:00 a.m. sharp. It was cold! Even with all the adrenaline pumping through my veins, it was January on a breezy island with a cold bib of water on my back. It was race time. I had zero negative thoughts. I was ready to rock and roll! I had no clue what I was about to experience.

I only had one goal for the race: run 50 miles in under 9 hours. For me this was doable. It would mean running an average of a 10:48-per-mile pace, which I thought was a good enough cushion, considering my normal pace. Normally, I would run a marathon with an average pace of 7:30 to 8:00 minutes per mile. Typically, running longer distances, you will slow your runs down, especially with the elevation gained during this run. In order to accomplish this goal, I had to follow my plan perfectly. But how—with my muscles not hydrated enough from the day prior? Still, I remained positive.

We started the run, with the first couple miles being fairly flat. Then there was a few thousand feet of elevation gain within a short few miles. There was some serious slope to this mountain we climbed. I ran the entire hill all the way up without stopping. Since I was well trained, it was not that difficult with the right pace. It was pitch black. You could only see the lanterns on everyone's head guiding their running path. I did not recall, on the way up, since it was practically a few miles straight up, seeing but a handful of people running up the hill. Nearly 95 percent of the runners were walking. Honestly, not a bad idea either. But that was not a part of my plan or mindset.

I have one general rule of thumb that I have always stuck to when running races: even if I am running at a snail's pace I never stop running. That is my one rule. Even if it is slower than a casual walker, I will not stop. For me, stopping symbolizes a mental defeat, which is not good for my running psyche. I never give up when I believe in something. For me, running is something that I do not always enjoy doing. Especially when it is painful. When it is painful, there is something exciting that happens. Although the body is failing, the mind has an opportunity to be strong and grow in the process. I love running long distances for that one reason.

Well, I finally made it to the top of the hill. I was at a stellar pace. My body and breathing felt exceptional. The beautiful terrain and views of the sun just coming up over the horizon were magnificent. I kept enough in the reserves to not make the mistake of pushing myself too hard. I had to make sure to finish the race in under 9 hours, so I kept my pace right around 10:15 per mile, saving a little breathing room for the end, in case I slowed down a bit. All of a sudden around mile marker 18, I felt a little bit of knee pain, which was absolutely not normal for me. I'd never had any issues before with my knee. Anytime I had any injuries, I would take the time to rehabilitate them, especially if it was a knee.

Regardless of the pain, I kept my pace. As each mile went on, the pain grew—to the point where at mile marker 25, I stopped to take a sip of water and feel around my knee to see what could be wrong. As soon as I stopped, my knee locked up on me. Instantly a shooting pain shot up and down my leg. This was so out of the ordinary for me. But I was not a foreigner to pain since I have had many injuries before. Tracking my race time, I was making the 25-mile turn running a 10:26-minute mile. That put me at 4 hours and 14 minutes for the first half. Remember, I was looking to finish in under 9 hours. I was well within my pace. Minus, I had a huge dilemma with my knee.

I sucked it up and attempted to run. But it was excruciating! I proceeded to do my best, but I could not run properly without excruciating pain for longer than 30 seconds. Determined not to give up, I ended up running on one leg. Of course, my other leg was present and acted as a crutch to help me with the impact. I literally single-legged it through the race. It was honestly one of the more difficult physical challenges I have ever met.

Not only was my knee in throbbing pain, but it was a mental battle, not knowing if I was permanently damaging my knee. To make matters worse, as one after another runner passed me by, it started to tremendously frustrate me. It pissed me off, knowing I was losing position after position. Obviously, I would, on one leg. But I am a highly competitive person, especially with myself. I started the race out front, one of those in the lead. Just over two hundred competed on that day, and I was slowly but surely finding myself in last place. But what did I expect?

At this point, I was in danger of not being able to finish the race at all. Although my goal was to complete the race in under 9 hours, the race gave you a cut-off time of 12 hours total. I was in a psychological battle to not give up. It had less to do with my pride, more to do with the possible permanent damage I was causing to my knee. Plus, I kept asking myself the question, "Why is this happening to me?"

The only logical explanation was that I was severely dehydrated, which ended up being the culprit in my meticulous analysis after the race. As I was battling my mind, I was, perhaps foolheartedly, determined not to give up. I would tell myself over and over: *You are not a quitter. You never give up. Keep going. Keep fighting.* I was in my last 13 miles, going through the backcountry of Catalina. There were multiple rangers driving past me, picking up groups of runners. They would always stop and ask if I wanted to be picked up. I would politely proceed with a "no thank you." They would then politely remind me that if I did not pick up my pace, they would be forced to pick me up. They would explain that the sun was going down, and I was in a natural reserve, which meant that part of the Island is closed to the general public. I would repeat politely that there was no way I was getting off this track.

There was no way I was going to finish on time, before they shut down the event. I had rangers on my butt about to attempt to kick me out. I was in my last 8 miles in the dark. Every time I heard a vehicle approaching, I would jump in the bushes. As I said, there was no way I was not going to finish that race. I did not care that I was not going to get an official finish time. I was going to cross that finish line. My knee was still in excruciating pain, and by this time I was finally starting to feel the fatigue of being out on the course for nearly 13 hours.

Ended up making it through the backcountry to the final home stretch, with only the last couple of miles to go. They were all downhill on an old asphalt road that was severely uneven. That was probably some of the worst pain I experienced all day. Trying to one-hop all the way down the mountain on the asphalt was painful, to say the least. Finally, I saw the finish line. I was belligerently tired at this point. The finish line was no longer lit up, with the timer showing the racers' finishing times. It was completely dark, with everyone celebrating behind the finish line, not paying attention to any oncoming racers. To be fair, the race had been shut down for a couple hours. Just at the finish line I saw my wife and two kids. They seemed tired from a long day of waiting for Daddy.

When I actually crossed the finish line, my wife asked me, "What happened?" I explained, and we both laughed. Life is comical that way. I ended up finishing in 14 hours and 1 minute. My last 25 miles, I ran at an 18:12-per-mile pace. My overall average pace for the 50.5 miles (0.5 was me jumping into the bushes) was a 16:39-per-mile pace. I had a total elevation climb of 8,400 feet and burned

10,100 calories for the race: not bad for a day's work. I finished with a sense of relief, ready to throw some ice on my knee.

I am so thankful I made those poor strategic choices that led to my race-day demise. Had I planned for my motion sickness, come out a few days early, stayed hydrated, and finished the race, accomplishing my goal, I would have woken up the day after and just moved on. Regardless of my successes in life, it has always been a never-ending process of accomplishing goals. Typically, I take little time to bask in my successes. It does not matter what I accomplished yesterday, as it does not apply to today. I do not relish my successes for too long. But since I'd just finished running 25 miles on two legs and another 25 miles on one leg, it was an accomplishment I was not going to forget about anytime soon.

It is one thing to think you are capable of being strong and believe at your core you can accomplish great things. But proving your strength and determination through real-life experiences, now that's a whole 'nother level of self-mastery. Only through testing your limits can you develop a perseverance that will endure all hardships. Plenty of people talk the talk, but not everyone leads by example in the end.

When you get the opportunity to feel the pain of success, I say relish it. Before you know it, the opportunity will pass you by. We all get chances to develop perseverance, but not everyone recognizes that pain as an opportunity to grow. Most people give up too easily. When you give up, you miss the opportunity to grow. Truly embrace your hardships and struggles, as those are blessings from God. People often pray to God for perseverance yet do not always realize that God has already answered their prayer through opportunities to *build* perseverance.

Whether you believe in God or not, we all have the freedom to choose our own path in this life. That's undebatable. It might be a rough path or a difficult choice, but we all have the choice to choose the right path or wrong. We do not always realize which is which.

Sometimes we have so many thoughts going around in our head that our vision clouds. Do not be led astray from the apparent truth that is right in front of your face. You want to become your authentic self? Then you will need to learn to develop perseverance, as life is going to beat you up. It all depends on how you respond to the fight life brings. Will you get knocked down and stay down, or will you get back up and have a never-quit mentality?

It is that mentality that will develop your perseverance. Building that tough skin will allow you to embrace the pain. Having the chance to recognize that pain is not always bad. God gave us pain so that we can experience growth. Pain is good. Pain is your friend. Pain leads to perseverance. Perseverance leads to an individual who never gives up. If you have decided to never give up, then you've decided to embrace pain as your friend. As a gift from God. Understand your pain and know why you experience it. Do not run from it, as it seeks to destroy you. However, you do not have to let that happen. The choice is yours. Choose a strong mentality, and you will persevere at all levels.

My race was a beautiful race. It's my favorite race, to date. I am thankful to have felt the pain of pushing past the temporal hardship, gaining a new badge of honor. To know that I am capable of persevering through my present struggles. I was the only one who could get me through that race. The only one who could prove I was not a quitter. I was the only one capable of not giving up. The only one capable of pushing past the extreme physical and mental anguish. On that day, I grew as a person. I knew myself on a deeper level. I am so thankful I chose right.

If I had not taken the time to be diligent about investing in myself, I would not have been physically and mentally prepared for that feat. When adversity strikes, that is when you know who you really are—when you find out whether you have really put in the time to know yourself: to understand who you really are. I believe it is so important to invest time in knowing what you bring to the table of life. Only through self-observation will you be given the opportunity to gain the strength that you need in order to accomplish anything in life. Mental toughness is first developed in your mind through persistent daily action towards knowing yourself.

People believe they know themselves, yet it is not evident through their life example. They do not invest the time to be present enough to know who they really are. Too many times, we see people around us who invest in the lives of those in and around their circle but do not put in the time with themselves. Yes, it is a beautiful thing to love your neighbor as God commands us to, but we are to love our neighbors as ourselves. Most people do not have a problem loving themselves. Even if you believe you do not love yourself, I believe you probably do.

Even with that love of yourself, are you investing enough into knowing yourself? And not a self-centered love that seeks only your ambitions, but a beautiful love that wants to be your best version so you can enhance the lives of those around you. You cannot truly help out those around you unless you can help yourself first. The first rule of an emergency situation is to help and protect yourself before others. Putting yourself in a situation where you are not fully equipped with the necessary skills and strength to provide help will only leave you failing in the end—feeling broken and unsatisfied. Let us equip ourselves with the perseverance to accomplish anything.

You might have a desire, like me, to change the world one person at a time—a big, beautiful goal. But have you spent enough time developing your perseverance to realize that goal? Well, I want to guide you down a path that will give you a practical way to accomplish the perseverance you need to realize your goals. The determination and willpower to push past all the challenges that lie ahead. Let us build the mindset and prepare our minds for future struggles.

It all begins with knowing yourself. Investing in yourself to be ready for those challenging moments. How do people know themselves? How do you know that you know yourself? Where does someone even begin? Well, it starts and ends with you setting aside the time. To build perseverance focus on the two P's: Preparation and Practice.

Preparation is all about getting ready. The key to your preparation is knowing yourself on a deeper level, with the ultimate goal of building up your perseverance so that you are able to weather the storms of life. These storms are for all different durations of time—short-lasting storms or extremely long storms of struggle. Prepare yourself by focusing on having quiet time with yourself. I know it sounds a little silly to have quiet time with yourself, especially since life is crazy, with all the moving parts. But set aside some time to be in a quiet place in your mind.

To do this quiet time daily, find a place that works for you. Decide on how long that quiet time will last. It could be for five minutes or fifty minutes. The point is, make the time; no excuses on this one. In your quiet time there are a few different tools you can use to help you: journal, pray, or meditate. Everyone is designed differently so you decide on the tools best for you. My advice is to focus on using one tool at a time. This will allow you to hone in on which tool works best for you.

Journaling is all about asking yourself questions. Think about meeting someone for the first time. What sort of questions would you ask to get to know them? Ask yourself intriguing questions. For example, what makes me happy? What makes me sad? What makes me nervous? What makes me excited?

From those questions you can ask deeper questions, depending on the response you give yourself—constantly diving deeper, past the surface level of your mind. The deeper you dive, the more you will know yourself. Being able to articulate your thoughts onto paper will only better serve your ultimate purpose of building perseverance. And remember, that is the ultimate goal.

And also pray. Especially when praying out loud, you are tapping into a different center in your brain that will allow you to process your thoughts. Our thoughts are not always clear. But when we can get them out of our mind and into reality, using words on paper, then we have a chance to be impacted on a deeper level.

If you believe in God, this will deepen your relationship with Him. God will bless you with new levels of understanding. This understanding will give you the wisdom and direction to know yourself more. God desires for you to know yourself as He knows you. You were perfectly created in God's image. Due to sin entering the world, we have damaged God's creation. We have made mistakes. I have made mistakes. We have lost perspective on God's design for us. It is His desire to know us and for us to know ourselves as well.

Meditating is a time to reflect on our lives—on the decisions we've made, whether good or bad. Not to dwell on the past so as to hinder us. But to realize why we made those decisions. In the first place, how could we have made a better choice if given another chance? If given the chance, we would decide to make a better choice. In your meditation, choose to focus in the way that best serves, knowing yourself. My recommendation is to think of one single thought and allow that to take you down a path of knowing yourself deeper. You will gain new levels of understanding. Also, think of absolutely nothing. Rest in a peaceful state of mind and just exist in that moment. This one is challenging for most people. It is not easy in the midst of life to think of nothing. Yet, it is possible. As I'm a mover and shaker—so I've been told—sometimes it's hard for me to sit still, let alone think of nothing. It has taken me time to learn this one, but I am now capable of it. If I'm capable of it, you absolutely are too. Trust me.

These tools will allow you to be prepared for the inevitable challenges just around the corner. If you are going through an easy season, then challenges lie around the corner. If you are going through a tough season, then an easier season is around the corner. Life has an ebb and flow. It's up to you to decide on how you will react to those seasons. These are all tools to prepare you for the future. Preparation may get you ready, but in Practice the real growth lies.

There is no better place to grow your perseverance than through real-life practice. The good news about this one is that you will have plenty of practice opportunities. Life is full of challenges for everyone. No one can escape the reality of these adversities. The key is knowing these challenges lie ahead. They will give you opportunities to practice your perseverance. Relish the easy opportunities to grow. Other times, these challenges will seem unbearable.

It is important that we do not run from situations that are seemingly unbearable. Seize the opportunities to practice in real-life scenarios with perseverance. Discover your perseverance thresholds. Understand your weaknesses, as we all have them. Do not fear challenges. Whether it's a difficult conversation you know you need to have or a decision whose consequences you know will be challenging, do what is right by running towards the challenges. Look them dead in the eye and face those fears. Be a titan for your ultimate goals. Persevere at all costs. Live a life worthy of admiration. Be an example of what is possible when someone puts in the work and never gives up on themselves.

Know that you can persevere so long as you believe you can. Do not quit on yourself. Believe in yourself and know that you are capable. Put in the preparation to know yourself deeper. Then when these real-life opportunities come your way, you will be ready to conquer those challenges. With a *never quit on yourself* mentality, you are in the driver's seat. In the driver's seat, you will build the perseverance you need to be victorious in the end. The end result will leave you feeling satisfied.

Now, how great would that be, to be at the end of your life—knowing that you persevered through all the life's challenges with max effort? Knowing that you tapped into every fiber in your body, mind, and soul to achieve your goals in this life? That you were relentlessly unstoppable? Achieving your goals is going to take constant perseverance. Put in the work to know yourself, to understand who you are at your core. Believe in yourself regardless of the challenges that are in front of you. If you never give up on yourself, you are a winner.

Fitness

The daily care a person chooses for their
body and mind—we only get one.

> Fitness is like brushing your teeth—
> it needs to be practiced daily.
>
> —*Anonymous*

My whole life, I have been an active person. I am forty years old now. I am what you call a mover. I can sit still and relax when needed, but I have always preferred to be in motion. I have to thank my mom and dad for setting a good example in this department. They both showed me what an active lifestyle looks like. Both my parents are busy bees, constantly focused on accomplishing the next task. Because of their example, I was never one to sit around, playing video games or anything else that was non-active. Thank you, Mom and Dad, for living out the example of an active life.

Though being active my entire life, I was not always into fitness. I did not even fully comprehend what fitness meant when I was younger. My first eighteen years, I was involved in sports. So I did not have to think much about doing fitness. When you are in your younger years, fitness is typically much easier. You do not have to make the time. Normally, for most kids it is natural to want to get outside and use their bodies. For others, that might not be the case, but needless to say, when you are younger it is easier to take care of your body.

When you are younger, you naturally have a faster metabolism, and your body is not affected by poor nutritional choices to the degree it is later in life. As you get older, they become more problematic, especially with the less-than-ideal quality of most available foods. With age, a poor food environment and lack of physical movement causes a lot of inflammation in the body. When inflammation sets in, in a snowball effect it is even harder to get the body and mind working towards making better choices. Poor choices lead you down a path that, once on it, is hard to get off. In the same way, good choices can lead you down a path where it's easier to succeed. Clearly, most of us need to make better choices.

As I stated, in my youth being active came naturally. It was not until I was eighteen that I became more aware of how important it is to take care of my body and mind. I started to learn a lot about how important—for my long-term physical and mental growth—proper nutrition and exercise really was. That's when I got into running and resistance training with various types of weights.

Initially, I was running nearly every day. I really enjoyed the meditative high I'd get from that time on the road. I was running between three and eight miles a day. I was so proficient at running that I would get up early, go for my run, and take ten-second power naps mid-run (true story) on days I was a little tired. Around my house I had a ton of trails mapped that I could literally run with my eyes closed. I would not recommend that, but that is how often I was running and most days really enjoying it.

Like other things in life, even when you are passionate about something, it is not always easy. One huge key to success with your fitness routine: do not base your fitness off feelings but only the discipline to be consistent. If we all lived our lives based on feeling, most of the greatest athletic accomplishments of all time would have never been achieved. Discipline is the key ingredient to consistency: maintaining an attitude that says, "regardless of how I feel, I know how important it is to take care of myself so I will do what I said I was going to do today." Take it one day at a time. One step at a time. If you must, inch your way forward. The point is, daily effort will be your key to long-term success.

Besides running, I was lifting weights about three times a week. I was not too passionate about lifting weights. But I knew the benefits. I would go down to the local YMCA and get my workout on. In the early days of lifting weights, I am sure it did not look pretty. I really did not know what I was doing. I simply, grunting with effort, picked up weights and put them down. No one mentored or guided me. I did not read any articles but simply showed up at the gym with the intent of getting a good workout. At that time, it was good enough.

When I was nineteen, I moved away to college in a small town of nearly a couple hundred residents. The only things to do outside were work out, hike, and fish. And when I say that was the only thing really to do, I mean it. I lived in Hume Lake near Yosemite National Park—sixty miles from the nearest city of any real population. We were in the Sequoia National Forest—extremely secluded—up on a mountain just over five thousand feet in elevation. Thankfully, they had a decent little gym. I attended it regularly. After being away from home for a couple years, I moved back to beautiful Orange County, California. I was twenty-one, excited to be home, with access to more fitness possibilities.

Up in the mountains it snowed heavily for more than half the year, so I did not run as much as I would have liked. I have never been a fan of running on treadmills, so I was not about to run inside the gym. So, once home, I got back into my old routine of running nearly every day, running marathons, and lifting weights about three days a week at 24 Hour Fitness.

Also, I got a couple of jobs. One at Costco doing every job under the sun. The other was volunteering with my church youth group. My plan was to become a pastor of a Christian church. I was convinced that's what I wanted to do with my life. At the same time, I felt uncertain. I knew I wanted to help people, regardless of my profession, but what was that profession going to be? The job at Costco was just to pay the bills. The job at the church was my passion. I absolutely loved working with youth. Yet, I was not 100 percent certain I wanted to be a pastor. I did eventually get hired on as a youth pastor for the church.

But I was still searching for something else. As I was working at Costco and the church, trying to figure out something new I could do, I started to jump from community college to community college. I went to Orange Coast College to become a chef. When I was younger, I'd worked in the kitchen as a prep cook, dishwasher, baker, server, and banquet supervisor. I really enjoyed it, so I thought that's what I wanted to do with my life. The program at OCC was in hospitality and hotel management, which would give me the qualifications to enlist in their culinary program. I ended up deciding it was not for me.

I also went to Santa Ana College to become a firefighter. They had a popular fire technology program. If you went through all nine classes, you could enroll to join their nationally recognized academy. I ended up deciding that was not for me either. Then, I went to Saddleback College, enrolled in their business program. That was short-lived, as I did not care for the school. I never cared for the traditional school system.

I was left not knowing what I wanted to do in life. I kept my head down and kept working towards something that I knew I would eventually discover. I took a long time to reflect on life as I was bouncing around from college to college, working both jobs. I realized that I was a bit of a maverick in my thinking, a free-thinking individual who wanted to be independent from the status quo. I did not see myself fitting into a box. Through much self-reflection, meditation, prayer, and time with God, I finally discovered what I wanted to be. I was in my early twenties. I wanted to be an entrepreneur.

The life of an entrepreneur was intriguing. It fits the bill for who I am. It was a life full of freedom yet risks that would bring about many future challenges. I have always loved a good challenge. I always love being told I *cannot* do something. I have always opted to do what I want to do, not what others tell me to do. Being an entrepreneur gave me the freedom to do what I wanted to do when I wanted to do it. Now I just had to discover what industry I was going to pit my lifestyle and life goals with.

One day, as I was working out at a 24 Hour Fitness in Irvine, California, the manager, Chris Long, approached me to praise my fitness transformation and positive attitude. Then he surprised me with a job offer. He asked me simply, "Have you ever thought about becoming a personal trainer?" It had never crossed my mind. We set up a meeting to go over the details. I loved everything about it! Plus, I liked the idea of working for Chris, who had an unbelievably motivating, positive attitude. Someone I respected who could mentor me. I am jumping ahead here, but Chris was quite impactful in my personal-training career. Ultimately, I ended up coaching for nearly two decades, and he was always someone whose enthusiasm and energy I aspired to mimic. Thank you, Chris, for being an extremely positive influence on my life.

Back to the story. Certainly, the idea of a one-on-one setting with an individual I could not only push physically but also, on a deeper level, connect with appealed to me greatly. I've always enjoyed relating meaningfully. It seemed like a natural fit. Plus, it had not been on my radar at all. I loved the radical idea of doing something that was completely out of left field.

Ever since I gave my life to Christ, July 15, 2001, I have always wanted to connect with people on a deep level. Always treasured knowing people . . . to really know them. Doing so would require a safe place to listen and understand them. It was not about preaching my beliefs but just love on people. God showed me His ultimate love by saving me. He loved me when I did nothing but curse Him. That love changed me. It has made me who I am. I am eternally grateful for my God and His love. He has given me the desire to show that same love to others even if I do not receive that love in turn.

I finally discovered what I was going to do as an entrepreneur: be a personal trainer. After getting my first certification and being mentored, I became one. My schedule got full within a month, since I wanted to help as many people as possible and make money in the process. I was extremely motivated. For the number of sessions serviced, I was one of the top-producing trainers in California at 24 Hour Fitness. I was even told on numerous occasions by my manager that I was not allowed to coach sixteen clients in a day. Coaching sessions at 24 Hour Fitness lasted one hour, so calculate that: sixteen clients equated to a sixteen-hour day. But I loved it!

I knew from the get-go that when the time was right, I would go off on my own and start a personal-training business. And eventually open my own gym. I was at 24 Hour Fitness for fourteen months and two locations before I decided to go out on my own, starting, in 2007, my first company, Elite Physique Fitness. I rented space from other local gyms. When I made the jump to go on my own, I was able to reduce my training schedule by 30 percent but increase my gross income by 300 percent. It was amazing! A huge blessing.

As the years went on, I continued to develop my craft as a personal trainer. I gathered over twelve national certifications as a nutrition specialist as well as in exercise science, corrective exercise, sports performance, proper prenatal care, and the list goes on. More importantly, I loved what I did so I put in the effort to learn how to become the best coach possible. For my clients. And consequently, I always had a full schedule of clients and good reviews to show for it.

It was not until March 2014 that I opened my first gym, Definition Fitness. To do that was not my initial choice. At the time I was renting space at a gym. The gym gave me and all the freelance coaches seven days to move their business somewhere else. It was going to be corporately owned instead of an independent franchise. That meant we had to get out.

Most of the coaches seemed to be panicking. Not me. I knew God had a plan. He would take care of me. So, a couple of good friends, Daymond and Desiree Sewall, and I got together to start a gym in the next seven days. Literally, in seven days we found a space in Laguna Hills, California, bought equipment—and opened, ready for business. It was not perfect, but under the circumstances it was an amazing accomplishment. My new partners and I knew how to handle business. We got the job done regardless of the timeline. We owned that gym for three years, until we relocated to a bigger space in the same city. Our first space was three thousand square feet, but we grew to need around five thousand square feet, which we ended up finding at the second site.

Two years later, I was ready for my next move. I'd always wanted to own a gym that I created from the ground up. In 2010, I came up with a unique concept I believed was going to change many lives. I ended up opening a third gym—B Body Fitness in Irvine, California. How the gym came about is for another book because it is a big, awesome story, but I will tell you this: we exclusively started to invite limited people to test the concept on May 7, 2020, right in the thick of COVID stay-at-home orders. This was California, remember. It was a crazy time to start a business, let alone in the fitness-and-service industry.

I am so incredibly grateful that I had the opportunity to be a part of such an amazing movement at B Body. We were able to help thousands of people during a very challenging time. It was a roller coaster that was incredible. A once-in-a-lifetime experience that will always be a season in my life to cherish. I relished all the challenges that came my way. I ended up selling off my interest in the company in September 2023. After being in the fitness industry as a coach for seventeen years and a gym owner for nine years, I was moving on to the next industry. My next endeavor was and is my real-estate company, Barrena Real Estate Group. But that conversation is for another time; now back to my point.

You might be wondering why I am telling you this story. I am simply telling you of my fitness journey and industry experience for one main reason. When it comes to fitness in general, I know what I am talking about. I speak from personal experience and have the educational background to help you live a better life by taking care of yourself through fitness. I am an expert in the fitness industry. Not just for the time that I clocked in, but for the blood, sweat, and tears I put into being my best for my clients over decades. One would think I left because I was burnt out. On the contrary. I still absolutely love it—helping people through their fitness journey.

Part of living an authentic life is taking care of your body and mind. Without a regular fitness routine, you will not be able to perform at your best. This is something I have seen most people neglect, even when extremely successful in other areas of their life. But their fitness and overall health is extremely poor. In turn they end up living shorter lives and inevitably do not feel as good as they could. It is top priority to make sure that how you treat your body is of utmost importance.

Whatever you consume that passes your jawline is going to affect how your body and mind functions. If you consume food of a poor nutritional quality, you will not think or operate at a high level. The physical stress you put on your body is also extremely important. Challenge your muscles and internal organs to work at a capacity that will allow you to function at an optimal level. You do not have to be a fitness fanatic to experience the overall benefits. There is a balance to gaining and maintaining your fitness.

I have been asked a lot of questions about fitness over the decades. Not just from my expertise in the industry but also because of my passion for my own personal health. To me, fitness has always been like brushing my teeth. I have to do it daily, multiple times a day. If you maintain your fitness every day, it is a lot easier in the long run to stay in shape. I never have to worry about conquering the mountain, as I am constantly maintaining a level of fitness performance. The question I'm most often asked is, "What is the number-one secret you have learned about fitness over the decades?" My reply is "Consistency is the key."

My answer is boring but extremely beneficial if applied to life. There is no secret formula. To stay consistent takes good old-fashioned daily effort. To achieve long-term success, the key is consistency. It does not always have to feel good or look pretty, but if you put in a daily effort to watch what you consume and move your body, you will win. You will find success moving in your favor. That momentum will allow you to experience the results that come.

Too often, we see people jump on the fitness bandwagon for three-to-six months and give up. They might even experience an amazing physical and mental transformation, but they very quickly revert. Some people go at it too hard. They are in it for the amazing transformation that impresses people and themselves. I mean no disrespect; that is a good accomplishment, but if you cannot maintain it for the entire duration of your life, you gave up too soon. Are you in it to receive adoration and feel good for just a phase of your life? Or do you want to be transformed forever? To have real, permanent, lifelong change, the key is consistency. Find a pace you can maintain for the rest of your life and never give up.

As with everything in life, there is an ebb and flow. Even when you maintain consistency, you can go harder in some seasons and other seasons go easier. The point: never go too high or too low to get you out of the game of consistency with your overall fitness.

Even though it is as simple as being consistent, there are important technical elements when it comes to putting together a routine that works for you. Well, you are in for a blessing today. Over the years I have created thousands of routines for clients and myself. My clients have ranged from Olympic and professional athletes to everyday sedentary people. It is important when putting together a strategic fitness routine to make the necessary adjustments to customize and tailor to the individual. Everyone is at a different level with their fitness. Some people are just starting out; others have much more experience under their belt.

I have created a unique fitness blueprint that, regardless of your fitness level, will potentially change your life. It will take some work on your part to answer the necessary questions in each blueprint step below, but when you are finished, you will have yourself a routine that will catapult you to success. Fitness routines can be complicated and too vigorous at times. Also, expensive. This one is extremely easy and repeatable for anyone who's ready to *take their fitness to the next level*.

Remember the Blueprint Habit. Let's return to it now. I love laying out strategy in a blueprint. So let's now tackle pointers for the Habit of Fitness. They will outline your fitness routine. We talked about the importance of a blueprint. Well, I'm laying this one out for you. It's simplified and easy to digest. A trainer could charge you thousands of dollars for it! True fact. But I am going to just give it to you for free. *The application is on you.* I really do want to see you succeed and find your authentic self. This will only be possible if you make your fitness as important as any other authentic habit. Be prepared to be diligent. Now, let us get to work.

FITNESS BLUEPRINT

❶ Set Game-changing Goals

Let's return now to Habit 1: laying the foundation, no matter what the desired outcome is, is always the first step in a blueprint.

In this case, that foundation is your fitness goals. Yours, and no one else's. What is it you want to accomplish with your fitness journey? Without goals you will be going directionless down a murky path that makes no sense. You will lose your way and ultimately go down in defeat. You really want to do some soul-searching on this one. Do you want to be able to see your abs? Or you just might want a flat tummy. Or you just might want to feel better. Whatever your goals, they must come from you, not outside.

Grab a journal to write all your goals down—both short- and long-term, and everything in between. Now, write them down in whatever order you feel is best. I start by writing long-term goals. Try to reach as far out as possible to discover exactly what you want your long-term goal to be. Even new to fitness, you might have a long-term goal to qualify and compete in the Ironman World Championship in Kona, Hawaii. That's an amazing goal, which will probably take you years to realize, depending on your current fitness level. But I still believe that goal is too short-term.

I want you to think so far out that you are visualizing your fitness goals on your *death day*. Notice, I did not say deathbed. Not everyone wants to die in bed. I do not. I am a mover and a shaker. I want to die standing up, embracing life to the fullest. So for me, one of my long-term fitness goals is to keep moving at all costs, no matter what. To never physically give up on myself. To fight to the death of my body. Now, that is one of my goals. You have to decide what it will look like for you to reach your ending days. Take some time to reflect on your long-term vision.

After you have written down your long-term goals, then backtrack all the way to the short term. Reverse-engineering your goals will allow you to better understand what it will take in the long-term. When you look at the bigger picture, you will go about reaching those goals at a different cadence. You absolutely want to reach your goals, but make sure they are maintainable and reasonable for your life. Do not go beyond what you are currently capable of. Yes, visualization is important, but if you have a hundred pounds to lose, and you are looking to compete in a physique competition in three months, you have probably aimed a little high and are being unreasonable.

I am all for being unreasonable and breaking the rules at times to set new standards for yourself, but only if they are reachable. Make the goals big—dream big—but also measurable. Once you have written down all your goals, you are ready to be let loose on your goals. When you discover your true authentic fitness goals, watch out, world. Your passion to pursue your goals will be unstoppable.

② Show Up for Workouts

Now, there are a lot of different ways to work out. Fundamentally, we want to put healthy stress on our muscles, bones, ligaments, joints, and organs. We are talking about healthy stress and resistance. The human body was meant to move, work, and utilize all its functions. It is through our sedentary lifestyle that we have created sickness in our bodies.

Let us break workouts into two categories: cardiovascular training and resistance training. Both have benefits that are pertinent to your overall health. You can decide how you want to get those two accomplished. Those can also progress and change in time. You can flip-flop, going back and forth between workout modalities. For me, these days my cardiovascular training is running trails, doing step routines, and striking a punching bag. Resistance training is lifting weights at the gym. I typically do cable or plate-weighted machines about 50 percent. The other 50 percent is with bar and dumbbell weights.

Personally, I break apart my workouts into body parts: full body, lower body, upper body, or core days. Every day is a little bit different for me. I try to listen to my body. Some days I will go harder than others. It all depends on what my body is telling me. That is a key to staying consistent: listen to your body. Now, for some people this can be a problem. They believe their body is telling them every day to not work out. That is not what I am referring to. I am saying that if your body is not feeling a particular exercise or body part *on that given day*, change it up. But definitely still work out.

Some people like the idea of joining local gym classes. Others might want to do Pilates, CrossFit, or kettlebell workouts. In my opinion, at the end of the day, it does not matter as long as you pick something that you do enjoy doing regularly. Once you find out what you would like to do for your workouts, now figure out how often. You should do cardiovascular and resistance training at least three times a week each. You pick the days—your choice. Perhaps do cardiovascular training on separate days from your resistance training or on the same days. Do what is best for your lifestyle, your body, and—most importantly—your peace of mind.

For me, I tell myself I am going to work out *every day at least once*. When I get to the point that my body feels like it needs a break, I take a break. Sometimes I work out for five days in a row; other times I go for twenty days in a row. It just depends on my life and how my body is feeling. Now, that's what I do. I am only giving you an example. You can choose to schedule your workouts however you please but do make sure to fit them into your life practically.

Everyone likes to work out at different times. I like to get up first thing in the morning and work out around 5:00 to 6:00 a.m. But only after my morning routine of praying, reading, and meditating–spending time with God. To me, working out early in the morning is like having my coffee. It wakes me up. But again, everyone is different. You might want to work out early in the morning but cannot, in view of your current lifestyle. That is absolutely fine. Find the time and make it happen. Not having enough time is always a poor excuse. It might be a good excuse because it is true, but you can always make the time. Make the necessary sacrifices, make fitness one of your top priorities.

Regardless of how you feel, do not base your fitness on feelings but on knowing it is the right thing to do for your long-term goals. Too many people live their life based on feelings. Fitness and feelings are two different things. In order to reach your fitness goals, you will need to maintain discipline regardless of how you feel on a given day. It is through game-changing goals that you will have the passion and drive to push past the feeling of not wanting to work out. We all have those feelings, but those feelings are not relevant to your long-term goals.

When you show up to your workouts, bring all of you. Give it 100 percent, based on what you have to give for that day. Some days your body will not be feeling it. On those days just do your best. Maybe throttle back a bit. The days you are feeling really good, go to town. Work hard. Show up to your workouts with the intention of focusing on bettering yourself. This will allow you to be more effective in life for others and reach your dreams.

③ Know Your Numbers

When it comes to nutrition, it is the single most important element of a complete fitness regimen. Dieting is something we all do, since what you eat is called your diet. You might not acknowledge your nutritional habits as dieting, but you are dieting. You either have a strict diet or a lucid one, but we all diet. It is important to know that your body and mind function based on the fuel that you give them.

If you feed your body and mind poor quality foods, your body will operate poorly.

My diet philosophy is simple: we all have similar functions with how our body works with various diets, but each body is uniquely designed differently. It is my belief that some people cannot process particular nutrients because of how their body is designed. We are not all the same. Everyone has been given a different machine. The idea is that you discover what tools work best for your machine. To illustrate this further, imagine what stands out in a sports car and what stands out in an off-road truck. Each design is completely different. The sports car is built for speed and precision, while the off-road truck is built for durability and strength. Both vehicles have similar functions, yet they are uniquely designed, with a different purpose in mind. Their engines are designed with similar parts, yet they perform best with different fuels. In the same way each human body is unique and requires different fuels to operate at peak performance. It comes down to balancing two things: your macronutrients and micronutrients.

Your macronutrients would be where you get your protein, carbohydrates, and fats. Macronutrients are your calorie source. I am not going to preach what macronutrient diet you should be on. As I have already stated, everyone has a different machine. For me, I have a high protein and high fat diet. I typically do not try to consume carbohydrates except through my proteins and fats. When I stay away from carbohydrates, I am able to steer away from most of the foods in my body that create unwanted inflammation. For me it is important to maintain my abs, aka the six-pack. Now, I know that that is not for everyone. But it is for me, it is important, so I watch my carbohydrate intake.

I typically do not have more than 80 to 120 carbs total a day. Sometimes I might have less and sometimes more, depending on what my body is telling me. Now, I have always had a flat stomach, but my six-pack did not come until I got into lifting weights in my early twenties. I am now forty and have maintained my abs for nearly two decades. That is a life goal for me. To keep my six-pack intact. It is a gauge to let me know whether I am making poor or good choices with my nutrition. It is not an obsession for me in order to be seen a certain way; I do not care what people think of me. It is something that guides me into maintaining a good diet.

I have noticed, as I got older, my body does not process food the way it used to. I used to be able to get away with poor quality foods here and there and still maintain a tight physique. Not so much anymore. As I left my twenties and entered my thirties and after, I had to be even more discriminating in food choices. I do maintain a high level of activity, which keeps my metabolism up. And as I age, my mind gets stronger, so it balances out: maintaining my physique takes me about the same effort.

Micronutrients are your vitamins, minerals, and water. Micronutrients do not possess calories. Micronutrients are all about eating the right foods. When you eat processed foods, you get minimal micronutrients. It is best to eat foods that are low processed. Low processed foods are typically whole foods; in other words, one-ingredient foods. Think of it this way: the food you consume will either energize your body and mind or slowly create illnesses. Remember that variety always deflects deficiency. Make sure to have a varied diet, which will provide different micronutrients that your body and mind need to function properly.

Do some research; try several diets and discover what works best for you. Remember, this is a lifelong journey. You should not be aiming for a quick transformation. This process, you have to commit to for the rest of your life. Slowly and consistently start to discover what diets work best for you. It is really about balancing your macronutrients and micronutrients. If you have the right balance, you will be calorically aligned with what your body and mind need to perform at their best.

4 Prepare for Everything

This is a hot topic. How do you cook food? Well, some people live an extraordinarily busy life, constantly on the go. If you fall into that category, you will probably need to prep your food in advance or hire a service to do that for you. Others have a slower pace of life. They can make each meal as they need the energy. There is no right or wrong answer for everyone. But there is a right and wrong answer for you.

The main point is to be strategic about how you prepare your food. And it must fit into your lifestyle. Decide what nutrients you need and plan out how you are going to consume them. You might need to be very methodical, prepping your food for the week. It is important to know as you go about each day where you are going to get your nutrients. If you do not plan ahead, you will find yourself looking for easy options. Quick, easy options—fast food or not—are typically not the best for you, as they are highly processed.

5 Track Your Success

In my opinion you can only have three general body-composition goals: lose, maintain, or gain. Even if you are trying to maintain your body, which is the easiest from a tracking standpoint, you will always have to do some analysis of the amount of food you are consuming. But if you are trying to lose fat or gain muscle, it will require some diligence in tracking your macronutrients and micronutrients.

Most people fail to journal their nutrition. If you have access to a smartphone, download a nutrition-tracking journal. This will allow you to know exactly what nutrients you are getting from the foods you are eating. It is important to know your calories, protein, carbs, fats, and all your micronutrients. If you do not have access to a smartphone, you still have options. Buy a small handheld journal in which you jot down the foods you consume. If you decide not to journal your food, you will still need—at the very least—to take mental notes of what you are consuming on a daily basis.

It is a given but not obvious that if you are going to be tracking your nutrition, you will also need to be weighing everything. Now, again, this depends on your goal and where you are at in your journey. For most people who are just starting out, they will need to weigh everything on a measuring device. Remember, this is only to help you down a path of *knowing exactly what you are consuming*. When you know exactly what and how much you are consuming, you will know how to make the necessary changes to maintain a diet that works for you.

6 Supplement the Missing

Unfortunately, due to the quality of the modern food process, we are missing vital nutrients daily. Even if you have all the money in the world, it is still hard to consume everything your body needs to be at an optimal level. That is why I highly recommend supplements to assist in filling in that gap. I am not going to tell you exactly what supplemental nutrients to take. I do believe there are a few key supplements that the body and mind require, which we typically do not get in our foods.

I consume multiple types of supplements for various purposes. I try to stay away from anything synthetic, maintaining a holistic supplement regimen. There are three top areas I believe the body needs supplements in. One: our vitamins and minerals, which are typically found in fruits and vegetables. Green shakes are a great way to get in your fruits and vegetables. Unfortunately, trying to consume the micronutrients that our body needs is nearly impossible without greens. Two: a joint support to help repair the joint damage inflicted in our various activities. Three: anti-inflammatories and antioxidants that will help prevent inflammation.

How we consume supplements is also extremely important. Digestion is a whole other big topic. There are multiple ways to take supplements. Research shows that the best, most reasonable way to consume supplements is in powder or liquid form. Typically, powder and liquids are more expensive due to the process of maintaining the integrity of the supplement. If you have the means, I recommend going with supplements that are in those digestible forms. Some supplements will not come in powder or liquid; at that point, I personally get soft capsules.

Before taking any supplements, you should always consult your physician. As I have stated, everyone is in a different circumstance with fitness. It is a case-by-case process of discovering what is best for your body. Supplements will help you fill in the gap of missing nutrients.

One of my friends, Dr. Calvin Ng, an excellent Natural Health Care Practitioner—at the top of his field—has a comprehensive approach, believing, as stated on the Cohn Health Institute website, that "all health dysfunctions have an underlying imbalance physically, biochemically, and emotionally." The human body is smart. It was designed to heal itself. Thus, to restore normal physiology, allowing "the systems of the body to function in harmony." He aims to educate others about the endless possibilities of holistic healing and inspire people to live a life to their fullest potential. That is why we are buddies. We are like minded. Highly recommend him.

7 Hydrate to Vitality

This is one of the single biggest things people neglect. They do not consume enough water. In turn, their bodies are not hydrated enough. I maintain a simple rule of thumb for myself: drink 1 ounce of water per pound of my body weight. I weigh 184 pounds, so I consume 184 ounces daily. And that would be at a bare minimum. Most days, I consume 200 to 300 ounces of water. Yes, you will be going to the restroom more often, but your body does adjust; you will get used to it. I go to the restroom once every hour.

The benefits of keeping your body hydrated are many, a long list. To name a few: increased energy, fat loss, muscle gain, improved skin quality, better vision, deeper sleep, increased stamina, enhanced brain processing, clear memory, and muscle recovery. The benefits are huge. Keeping your body well hydrated is of paramount importance. It is like keeping the right levels of oil in a car. Though cars are quite sophisticated and have thousands of moving parts, nevertheless. Try not keeping a car well oiled; that car will break down and not last long. Your body works the exact same way. Keep your body hydrated, and you absolutely will feel the benefits.

8 Manage Your Stress

Managing your stress is another a key element to your overall success. First, managing the stress on your body. Throughout the day you put your body in positions that are not ideal. If you are doing your workouts, you are also adding physical stress on your body—good stress, but it does take a toll on the body. It is important to allow your body to recover from all that stress.

You can do that in multiple different ways. To relax your muscles and elongate them you can do static stretches. Static stretching is hold-stretching for at least thirty seconds. This is best done at the end of the day, as it puts your muscles at rest. I have done a daily full-body-stretching routine for nearly two decades now. Over the years I have changed it up, but since it works for my body, I have not changed it much. No reason for changing something that is working.

Also, there are multiple different active release techniques to break down the tissue in your muscles. You can simply go to a massage therapist and get deep tissue or do muscle therapy called SMR (Self Myofascial Release) yourself at home with some rolling tools. I myself have about ten SMR rolling tools at home. I have others I take with me, traveling. My routine is to, at least a few times a week, do muscle recovery through SMR rolling.

I have a general rule of thumb that will help you with your muscle therapy. Now, I have stuck to this rule of thumb for decades. I have been able to prevent injuries and recover from injuries fairly quickly. For every hour that I put extreme stress on my body, aka working out, I put one hour into some form of muscle therapy, whether that be stretching or massaging and breaking down muscles. It might be a bit extreme for some people, but that's the way I've kept this flexible, injury-free body for the forty years of my life. That says a lot considering all the extreme sports I did over the years I've had thirteen broken bones, over thirty muscle sprains, ruptured discs, and other injuries. It says a lot about the importance of managing your body's stress. Too many people neglect muscle stress, not putting in the time to recover, and consequently, eventually, they get injured. Put in the time to recover from all your muscle use.

Fitness is not just about working out and dieting. In order to transform or maintain your fitness, you need to learn techniques to reduce your mental stress. We all know it is a fact that chronic stress is a killer—"linked to six leading causes of death including heart disease, cancer, lung ailments, accidents, cirrhosis of the liver and suicide, according to the American Psychological Association."[1] The main problem is, most of us do not know how to manage mental stress, where external circumstances invade our internal thought processes. What does one do, in that case, to alleviate mental stress? Below are some suggestions.

You can do any of the following: pick up a good book, learn something new, spend alone time with yourself, do focused meditation, pray out loud, begin a new hobby, get some good sleep, or get plugged into a community. All of these have one common thread: they allow you to depressurize and spend time doing what you love to do. Sometimes life beats us up. We spend plenty of time doing things because they pay the bills or are "the right thing to do," but at some point you need to do *what you want to do*. Doing what you are passionate about will energize you and alleviate your stress levels.

❾ Adopt a *Never Give Up* Mindset

You are your worst critic. You are the only thing holding yourself back. Without the right mindset, you will not likely reach your goals. *Do not be your own worst critic.* Get out of your own way. Make a conscious choice to think positively. Even if your circumstance seems daunting or impossible, with the right thinking you can accomplish anything. Have a *never give up!* mindset. You will win as long as you never give up on yourself.

❿ Consistency Is the Key

This fitness blueprint is everything you need to accomplish your fitness goals. The only thing that could get in the way is you. Consistency is the key. I start and conclude this chapter with that thought.

Be consistent even when you do not feel like being consistent. Keep your eyes on the prize. Even when you cannot see a clear outcome, take one step at a time.

Be intentional. Do not just coast through life. Put in the work and you will get the results. Fitness is not something to be mastered; it is simply something to be consistent about—on a daily basis. Your new authentic self will thank you if you stay the course. Remember, in fitness, consistency is everything. Even if it does not feel like you are making progress, you are if you stay consistent.

Once you understand this fitness blueprint and apply it to your life, you will be ready for the finishing touch. It is commitment time. Most people fear commitment, but not you and not right now. If you are ready to transform your life and follow this fitness blueprint, then it is time to commit 100 percent to your fitness for the rest of your life. However many days you have left, you will commit to taking action and focus on your fitness daily. It will not always be easy or look pretty but will be worth it.

The average person around you is out of shape and dissatisfied with their body, but you will be content and happy with what work you put in to take care of yourself. It is not just about looking the part but also about feeling the part. Feeling like you can climb any mountain that you set your body and mind to. It does not matter what your fitness goals are; it only matters how you will accomplish those through your determination to finish strong. Be the victor—never give up on yourself—because if you do not quit, you are a winner.

Community

The family a person chooses

> Alone, we can do so little; together
> we can do so much.
>
> —Helen Keller

I was blessed to have met the love of my life and best friend on January 19, 2006. After our first date, I knew this girl was different. We fell in love almost immediately. Sounds crazy, right? Well, I told her I loved her after only three weeks of knowing her, and the feeling was reciprocated, as she told me she loved me too. We had been dating for eleven months, and on December 21, 2006, I proposed. She said, "YES!" I would have liked a short engagement, but we finally got married September 20, 2008. It was certainly one of the best days of my life. She is my best friend. She is my beautiful bride, whom I love immensely. I have chosen to lay down my life daily and commit to her for always and forever.

Fifteen years later, I love her more today than I did the day we first met. More than the day I committed my life to her. She is far from perfect, but she is perfect for me. We balance each other out.

She is different from me in almost every way. We come from different backgrounds. We have led different lives. As I told you earlier, I like structure. That's true, but I am also spontaneous. And definitely outgoing. She is more of an introverted person, who thrives in a level of consistency and comfort. I thrive on a degree of chaos and change. I love it that we are so different—that we love each other so deeply, that our commitment is our most important reminder to be our best for each other.

Over all these years we have faced many struggles. Not necessarily in our marriage, but in the ups and downs of life. We experienced heartache and difficulty. It is so incredibly special to have someone by your side, regardless of the challenges. We have always had each other's back. My wife and I recognize that we have not always had this amazing marriage, but we have learned to work together as a team to make course corrections to learn from our past. That one is a never-ending process. We are always trying to better ourselves for each other. Especially, after we threw a couple kids into the mix, this one brought even more challenges to the table.

As I stated, I am an extrovert, constantly engaging with people. These people can be good friends, acquaintances, or strangers I just randomly run into. I thrive off building personal connections that can last a lifetime. Now, I do not get along with everyone, but I do get along with most people. I try to be authentic and genuine, candid and vulnerable. I try to be my genuine self. My authentic self. That has allowed me to build meaningful connections with more people than less.

It is my firm belief that when you are authentic about who you are, it will attract the type of people who are authentic and similar to you. This is immensely important. That way you will find your people. You will have the same interests and hobbies. You will have the same beliefs and values. These will be easy relationships to maintain, and not difficult, challenging ones.

For me this has led to a lot of built connections over the years that I am incredibly grateful for. *You know who you are.* How do you know? *Because I remind you often.* I love it that I have so many connections with people of all walks of life. I am thankful for these people I call my community. Community is so tremendously important. Community not only allows us to engage with people but also allows us to be ourselves.

When we associate with people who share our beliefs, we are challenged and grow as individuals. Better yet, when we associate with people who do not have our beliefs, we are stretched even more. It is important to have people in your life who are similar to you, but if you want to grow and be challenged, as I do, you will need to be around people who think differently from you. I believe this is beautiful. I love it that God has created us uniquely different. God did not make a mistake with you or me. God is intentional and has a plan for your life. He cares for you.

Part of that plan is community. We all have people in our lives with whom we can connect, but it is not always easy to know these people. You might need to step out of your comfort zone. You will not regret it. You will grow in the process and be blessed by those you encounter. Just think of the deep connections still out there waiting for you. These deep connections will change your life. We have all been born into a family, but we also have the family we choose. Go out there and choose your family. Choose wisely and put in the effort to these people.

Challenging the way we think, other people allow us to think outside the box. Not one person understands everything there is to know in life. Everyone brings a different set of experiences and knowledge to the table. That allows us to see life from a different perspective. If you believe that life is monotonous, maybe it is time you meet someone new.

When I said I am always meeting new people, my wife, on the other hand, is one to keep to herself. She draws her energy from spending time with herself and only the closest loved ones. My wife has a very tight circle, with not many people in it. But she has a deep connection with each of them. My wife is also far from shy. She just naturally keeps to herself. She has a different perspective on the community she chooses to engage with. I admire her feelings and understand her approach, which is not my approach. I am drawn to people. She is not drawn to people.

I believe there are pros and cons to both personality types: extrovert/introvert. There are some things I have learned from my wife and implemented into my life. As well, my wife has done the same thing on her end. I have observed that my circle has become big, to the point where it is nearly impossible for me to maintain all of these relationships. Yes, I am connected to a lot of people, but my question to myself is, *how many of these people am I truly close with? How many of them have I decided to make a part of my chosen family?*

As I stated, we have all been born into a family, whether we like that family or not, but we also have the choice to choose close individuals we connect with on a deep level. People we trust, whose back we have. They trust us and have our backs. We know they are on our side, and we love them for it. We all need people in our corner, fighting for us. People who have at heart our best interest.

Regarding my wife, she has deep connections. But she does not actively seek out new people, which means she misses out on opportunities to engage with others. Arguably, when you do not engage with new people, you are not being challenged enough. Meeting someone for the first time takes effort. In most cases, not a vigorous effort, but the effort of asking questions and putting in the work to know somebody you just met. New people give us new outlooks and possibilities. But it is also time-consuming and potentially energy draining, depending on the person.

That is why I love it that my wife and I are opposites in this authentic habit. Through personal observation, I have noticed I can work on knowing fewer people. Sounds selfish in my mind, but I have noticed that as I put effort into meeting new people, it takes away from the deep connections of those who already exist in my community. I have realized that if I do not put in the effort to maintain a relationship, I will slowly lose that connection. Through my wife's example, I've been led down a path of desiring to maintain the current community I have. That community is filled with close friends I call family, plus my blood family, that I want to be in close communion with as well.

On the other end, my wife has learned to engage with numerous new people. She has stretched out her comfort zone as she has seen me over the years learn how to engage with less people. It is a beautiful seesaw. I am still my outgoing, spontaneous self; my wife is also her reserved, exclusive self. But we have learned to be challenged in what is not natural for us. It is not natural for me to not engage with people, as it is not natural for my wife to engage with people. It is not natural for me to be reserved and replenish my energy that way, as it is not natural for my wife to be outgoing and charge her energy that way.

I am thankful for my beautiful bride. She is my opposite. I am her opposite. That apposition brings us a balance that I deeply cherish. Yet even though my wife and I are opposites, we have many core values and beliefs that make us united. Though admittedly, marriage is not for everyone, when you can find someone who you decide you want to commit the rest of your life to, it is absolutely beautiful in my eyes. There is no greater joy and challenge at the same time than marriage. It is the ultimate community. One could call it the ultimate challenge. To be in community with someone you give your everything to. Who you get to commit your heart, mind, body, and spirit to. You are literally becoming spiritually one with this person. It is a game changer. It is an ultimate life changer.

Building a successful community must start in your home. Someone I admire who portrays this quality, ascribing his roles as husband, dad, and grandfather, as primary to him, is entrepreneur

Doug Fields—an author of over fifty books, a speaker, and for many years a pastor. Most importantly Doug has built a strong community in his home. Having an evident passion for helping others achieve a strong marriage and an overall healthy family dynamic, he leads by example. Without people of influence like Doug, who demonstrate a good example, it would be hard to believe it is possible to create a solid community in our homes, considering how, in this day and age, life is riddled with broken families. Doug has many good books on this topic, but my top two recommendations would be the enduringly popular *7 Ways to Be Her Hero* and—also a good read—*Intentional Parenting*.

My main point—find someone in your life who has a healthy community within their home: a strong marriage, intentional parenting, and all in all good family life. If possible, ask that person what it takes and simply mimic the answer. This will act as your guide to cultivate a strong community within your home. Then you will be ready to build your community beyond.

This life is full of inconsistencies. It is sad to see all the brokenness and pain that exists in this world. It hurts my heart to see the disconnect. People long for people. Some want to change the world, yet do not know how to accomplish that mission. I can tell you that you cannot change the world unless you change lives. People are what make this world go around. People make this world beautiful. Imagine what kind of world it would be if you removed all the people on this Planet Earth.

You can find community everywhere. The point is that you establish community. People are necessary in our lives.

Without being challenged by those in your community who can introduce you to what you do not know—people who have a different viewpoint and set of experiences—you will not be able to discover your authentic self. I have a good friend named Chris Paliska, a great example of a leader who has cultivated diversity, fostering close ties in his workplace. Chris, an entrepreneur, owns a mortgage company, Total Quality Lending. He has built a strong loyalty among his employees, who are united in carrying out the same mission—to serve their clients and each other to the best of their abilities. They each bring a different set of skills, knowledge, and experience to the table. That diversity has allowed them to become one of the top companies in their industry.

Some of the best companies ever created, those that have gone the furthest, depend on their team members thinking differently, yet they are united by one common mission. Being challenged by people who do not think exactly like us allows us to grow and accomplish great things together. There is an old African proverb that says, "If you want to go quickly, go alone. If you want to go far, go together." That diverse unity draws us closer and allows us to go much further together.

By pouring your knowledge and experience into others, you will challenge them as well. They will then get an opportunity to grow. This life is not just about us and our personal development. It is about giving back to others, challenging them in the way that we want to be challenged.

This authentic Habit 6, of building community, is a key to your overall development. You can meet these people anywhere and everywhere.

It might come naturally for you to be outgoing and meet new people. If so, you, like myself, might want to consider how deep and meaningful your relationships are. Consider the thought that it is not about how big your circle is but rather how deep and meaningful those ties are. I challenge you to question your relationships. Take a healthy deep dive to ask who is in your community.

Are they impacting you in a positive way or a negative way? Are they challenging you? Are you challenging them? What are they providing you? What are you providing for them? How can you improve those connections? How can you challenge those connections to grow? Do not just coast through life, meeting people or not at leisure; be intentional.

Put in the effort to connect. To understand them. To sympathize with them. Build long-lasting, meaningful connections that can be life-changing for everyone.

Do not make it about building your network of people, but realize it is about building deep, meaningful connections. If you are like me, I would challenge you to know fewer people. Decide who you want to have in your close circle. It is still good to continue meeting new people. At the same time, realize that it is not about the number of people you know but about the people you have deep connections with.

Engage with them on a regular basis. Stay involved. Relationships are a two-way street. Show them you care by being present when they need you.

If you regularly keep to yourself, it might be time you step out of your comfort zone. If it is hard for you to connect, hard to find people you have common interests with, start with the basics. The basics are we all have one common interest, we share life together. We all have basic needs and a desire to breathe and live this life as we please. We all want to live and exist for another day. We can rally and support each other, based on such simple recognitions as that we all value life. Life is short and not always sweet; it demands community to support us.

To go through the ebb and flow of life with people you connect with in your community is only going to enhance God's original design for your life. Those connections will challenge you at the times you need to be challenged. One of the individuals I've made a connection with is Anthony Geisler, a good friend and mentor to me. Anthony is the CEO of a publicly traded company named Xponential Fitness. Over the years, he's been an overall sounding board to hear my thoughts and contribute his advice; a reliable, significant asset for me. Not just because of who he is on paper but because of who he is as a person. He has challenged me through his example of work ethic, perseverance through adversities, and dedication to excellence.

Without people in our community like Anthony, we will not be challenged. Thank you, Anthony, for being an exceptional friend and mentor I can consult.

People too often run from being tested; run from being confronted; run from adversity. We need to run toward them, realizing that challenge is where growth lies. I am just another person in your community who cares for you. Maybe we have never met, but I am in your community.

You picked up this book for a reason. And that reason is that you want more out of life. You want to find your authentic self. This authentic self is going to come with work and effort. That work and effort is going to be challenging sometimes. Just remember that where that challenge lies, growth is just around the corner.

There is no time like the present. You have been given a life and that life is finite. You are only guaranteed right now. Decide you want to put in the work to build your chosen community.

You want to engage with people who are in your circle and not in your circle. Actively work on the relationships you already currently have. Pour into those relationships. Dive deep into those relationships. Maybe some of those relationships are not the best connections for you. Move on from those people. You know the unhealthy relationships I am talking about. The ones that just bring you down. If you cannot add value to that relationship and grow, allow that individual or group to find community somewhere else. Remember, it is about you and it is about them. If there is no benefit on either side, then that relationship will only bring you down.

On the other side, there are people waiting to meet you. There are communities that need what you have. You have gifts and talents. Find those communities because without you those people will be missing something. And that something is you! You are valuable.

Enhancing other people's lives with your life will not only fulfill them, but it will bring you the greatest satisfaction. That satisfaction stems from a selfless love. That love stems from a place of laying down your life for others. To be there for others. To encourage others. They might not act like it, but they need you. We all carry around a level of pride that conveys to others that we have it all figured out. News flash: we do not have it all figured out. We are all incomplete without a community of people around us who love and support us.

That love is pure selflessness. Find your authentic self by building a community of people who are your chosen family. The choice is yours, and the time is now. You are only guaranteed this very second. Use it wisely, my friend. Build your community.

Selflessness

*Person who puts others as their top
priority before their own self-gain*

> Do nothing out of selfish ambition or vain
> conceit. Rather, in humility, value others above
> yourselves, not looking to your own interests
> but each of you to the interests of the others.
>
> *—The Apostle Paul*

A s long as I can remember, I always wanted to be a father. It was a dream. Even in my first life, when I was lost and reckless, I wanted kids—no matter that I was headed down a dark path, bound for a straitjacket. When God transformed my life and I found my firm foundation, I desired to have kids even more. I think there are multiple reasons why. Mainly, I loved the idea of establishing a legacy in my kids that could live on after I die.

This chapter, I'm using the example of being a parent as a lesson in Habit 7, selflessness, while recognizing not everyone has, can have, or wants to have children. That's OK: there are plenty of other situations where selflessness is required. But permit me to continue using parenting as an example of learning to be selfless.

Having kids radically shifts your perspective on life. I am convinced it is one of the most amazing things anyone can experience on Planet Earth. My kids are my world. My kids are where my legacy begins. You see, we waited until I was thirty-three years old to have them. Even though I deeply desired kids when I was younger and even more so when I changed my life at around eighteen, I knew it was impractical. First, I had to find my love, which I did. My wife is the keeper of my heart.

There is a level of indebtedness when having a child. I am sure you have heard it said before, it takes two to create life. I believe it takes three. One capable man, one courageous woman, and one all-powerful God. Those three create life. And what a beautiful life that is. Life is so precious. Children are so precious. It is hard to debate the beauty of having a child. A life that you are privileged with for nurturing, caring, providing, mentoring, and teaching it how to live. I am indebted to God for my beautiful children, whom I love dearly. Only God can create something so perfect.

My children have had a huge impact on my life. They have taught me so much about myself and life in general. Without them, I would not have the perspective on life the way that I do. My goal is to be these three roles with my children—Father, Friend, and Mentor. It is a constant juggling act. I am not always perfect as a father. I learned that from them. It is nearly impossible to be a perfect parent. Being the perfectionist and highly motivated individual that I am, I want to be a perfect dad. I can now say, after having two children and being a dad for nearly eight years, the perfect parent does not exist.

My goal in trying to be the Father, Friend, and Mentor to my children is to do my best every day. Every day is different. As my children grow, I am forced to grow with them, or, I have realized, I am left in the dust. My children are constantly learning. It reminds me of growing up and going through the similar emotions they experience daily. As you know, my father was not always in the picture. That created an immense desire in me to be present in my children's lives. I want to be not just physically present but also emotionally, spiritually, and physically engaged. I do not always achieve this one, but I try to do my best. Still striving to be that perfect dad.

It is my desire to be engaged with my children. I am not going to lie; this one is really hard for me. I am highly ambitious, as I know my calling. I carry a weight on my shoulders to change the world. I know that begins with my children. How am I to change the world if I cannot influence my children in a positive direction? Quite often, I ask myself that. Naturally, I am systematic. An organized individual. With time I've learned to be intentional and disciplined with my actions. That has taken a lot of growth.

I constantly need to remind myself to not just be in the same room with my children but to engage. It's so easy to get tired and beat up from this life. I do not always give my kids what I know they crave—a fully present daddy. If you are a parent, you understand what I'm talking about. I could spend a good amount of time with my kids on a daily basis but not be present the way I want, the way they need. *Why?* you ask. Because this life holds many distractions with many burdens. Even the many blessings serve as a distraction. Distraction takes us away from the things that are right in front of our face. Our children being one case in point.

I believe it is healthy to carry a load on your shoulders that helps you realize the importance of your role as a parent. We all know life is finite. It is so tremendously short. Just think of all the generations that have come before you and that will go on after you. You are a vapor in the scope of human history. Placing a legacy in our children allows us to live on in them. To me that carries a weight that I am reminded of daily. I want to do my best for my children. I want to show them what it looks like to lead an abundantly blessed, fulfilling life.

This life does not rule us. But we can rule this life. I tell my children that they are the boss of their lives. They can make whatever choice they want, but they had better be ready for what comes next. As we make choices, those choices will have outcomes, whether we like them or not. It is important that we live in the present in order to focus on the future.

Why am I going on about being a parent when this habit is about selflessness? That's a good question that I want to unpack with you. First and foremost, being a good parent requires selflessness. Keywords here, "good parent" (not a bad parent). There are good parents and there are bad parents (even though there are no perfect parents). There is no in-between in my mind. If you want to be a good parent, involved in your children's lives, it's going to require selflessness. As parents, we have our own desires, which is good, but we often must deny ourselves for our children.

That's another thing I've learned from my children—to deny myself. In our house, our children do not always get their way. We are clear with them that it is not always about them. Sometimes Mom and Dad want to do what we want to do, and if you don't like it, tough. Life is black-and-white in this regard. You do not always get what you want, so better start learning at a young age.

I have these quotes with my kids that I've come up with over the years. One I use quite often is, "If you want to be first, be prepared to be last." I want my kids to understand *it is not always about being first in life. Actually, if you really want to be first, then you have to be prepared to be last.* Jesus taught me this. It is about denying yourself and allowing others to go first. It is human nature to want to be first. To have the spotlight on us. To be recognized, admired. We want *what we want when we want it.* To a certain extent we all have a child's mindset. That is exactly how a child thinks from birth. No one had to teach us to desire to be first. We knew that from the get-go.

The interesting part is that if we desire to be recognized and acknowledged in the spotlight, we must put others first. Being selfless in this regard is one of the most difficult things to do consistently. No one, and I mean no one, does this naturally. From Mother Teresa to Gandhi to Tony Robbins—every great person must learn self-denial. Though not easy, it is possible. Like most things in life, it takes daily effort. Once you learn how to put others first, you will constantly need to remind yourself to live out that choice.

When my kids look at me, I want them to see a man who denies himself for others. A man who puts others before himself. A man who puts his family before himself. A man who puts his God before himself. That is one of the legacies I want to leave. I want them to have a good example of a man who did everything he could to help other people. I cannot take credit for this, for it is my God who has instilled this passion in my heart. A passion to see people be recognized and win in life. To see people live their best life. I have gifts, talents, and abilities that I try to utilize to help people, but even if I do not possess what it takes to help someone, I am always willing to try.

My heart for people is a heart that is not my own. My Savior rules my heart. He gently invades my mind and soul to help the lost. The broken and abandoned. The people who have been neglected and forgotten. The bedraggled and beaten. These are my people. *Why?* you ask. Because none of that is true about them. There is a God who loves them. A God who has neither forgotten nor abandoned them. I am only a messenger, who is compelled to share the good news of what life could be like with Him. You see, if it were not for my God, you would not be reading this passage. Or this book at all. There would be no book. There would be a faint memory of a boy who could have been a real man. Who could have lived an extraordinary life, but he *chose himself.* Christ saved me. For that I am eternally grateful to Him.

This life is not about us. This life is about others. Think about anything that you could possibly achieve in this world. Typically, we associate possessions with success—fancy cars, beautiful homes, nice clothes. You know that list goes on and on. Well, let us flash forward to the end of your life. It's your death day. You are reflecting on the life you've lived. Reflecting on all you possess. You realize, in that moment, you are bringing nothing with you: no fancy cars, beautiful homes, nice clothes. None of that are you bringing on your journey. You realize you are all alone.

But you are leaving behind a legacy. When you think about it, that legacy is not in physical possessions. It is all about people. People make the world go round. Extract all the people from Planet Earth and how great the loss would be! What is the point of that planet? Think of all the meaning we add.

You might be asking yourself, *where do I even begin?* First and foremost, start with your community. And then beyond, expand to other communities. Being selfless is a huge step in building your legacy. People do not want to work with people who make it all about themselves. People want to work with people who want to help people first and foremost. Through selflessness you will discover yourself at a new depth. Isn't that crazy? You will discover yourself through serving someone else. You will learn more about yourself from others than you will from yourself. Deny yourself and you will lead an exceptional life, serving others.

It all seems overwhelming to deny yourself. I mean, I know it starts with my community, but what do I do? What does it even look like *to deny myself?* These are practical questions. These are questions that might sound silly to some, but most people have lived lives all about themselves, so they do not know what it looks like to think about others. I am telling you right here it starts with you making a conscious choice to put others first, before yourself. Start with one person and go from there. You want to change your family dynamic? Start with one person in your family. You want to change your community? Start with one person in that community. You have big goals of changing the world? Starting with one person is how it begins. Selflessness starts with one person at a time.

Cultivating selflessness is a daily choice to wake up and put others first. *Now, this does not mean you get walked all over.* This does not mean that you do not get your way sometimes. There are times when you will be the number-one priority but not nearly as often as we make it out to be. Most people are 99.9 percent all about themselves and 0.01 percent about others. Do the math; it adds up. Make it 100 percent about others and 100 percent about yourself. You need to focus on you so that you can be your best version for other people, but we also need to put our focus on other people, as they are dependent on our help. I say, if you can help, then help. Lend a hand to those in need.

There are people out there right now who are in a tough situation. Get out there. Find these people and help them. Without you, those people will have no help. You are their help. Do not just do this for the people in your circle. Serve people who challenge you outside of your circle. Of course, it will not be easy, but that's an opportunity for personal growth. Sometimes you need to put yourself in challenging situations to learn from that experience.

One of my friends, someone I admire, saw a need in her community. She is Autumn Strier, the co-founder and CEO of Miracles for Kids. Miracles helps families with critically ill children fight bankruptcy, homelessness, hunger, and depression—so they can fight for their kids' lives. For nearly two decades, Autumn and her team at Miracles for Kids have been a resource for families in crisis throughout Southern California and beyond, running financial-aid and other basic-needs programs to provide long-term aid to over fifteen hundred families with children battling over a hundred different life-threatening diseases. It started with a thought, progressed into implementation, and now is an organization impacting thousands of lives. Sometimes it is as simple as identifying the need in our community and taking a step towards solving the problem. People helping people is a beautiful thing.

This book is all about you finding your authentic self. You will have a difficult time finding your authentic self if you are making it all about you. Yes, this book denotes self as an emphasis, but to help other people is a way to focus on you. This is how we find personal fulfillment and help other people find their personal fulfillment. You have skills, talents, and abilities, so go out and use them for good to help those in need. It is not always about making money. Remember, money is something you do not bring with you when you die. Changing someone's life is something you bring with you when you die. It will influence that person's life forever and even their family generations to come. You could alter the course of history from just a simple act of kindness.

Just think: you have a chance to instill your legacy in hundreds and thousands of people. Better yet, you have a chance to instill your legacy in millions of people. I do not know about you, but I am fired up right now! I am looking to change the world. I am looking to make a difference in people's lives, as that is where I can instill my legacy. I do not want to build my legacy in things that fade away but in people who can impact people who then impact people. I want to send a ripple effect that will change the course of history. That begins with one person. It seems like an overwhelming and daunting task to change the world, but I assure you it is possible. I love that I get to tell you this when I myself have not changed the world, yet. Mark my words, I am on a mission to impact this world for the better. Join me and rescue those who want to be rescued.

I do not care to help the people who have it all figured out. Those people are good. They are taken care of, right? I am out to help those who want help. If I am capable, I am there. I want to serve and love those who need the support. I want to relentlessly bless the lives of those who need blessings. I want my children to see that their dad did everything for people before himself. I want my kids to know they are my priority, but other people come next, as they need us to help them. I do not know about you, but I know I do not see enough people standing up. I am not OK with it. People can choose their own life and I respect that, but we need more people standing up to do the right thing. To simply help people in need. As you will see illustrated later in this chapter, I personally did something about the need I saw in my community.

It is time to be selfless, get out there and make a difference. Do it with no strings attached. Simply deny yourself and serve. Help anyone and everyone who needs help. If you see a need yet do not understand how to fulfill that need, find someone in your community to help you. For example, someone I met randomly told me their friend lost their job and was looking to jump into a new industry, one I was quite familiar with. I was able to contact the individual, give them sound advice about the new industry of choice, and put them in contact with a possible job opening at my friend's company. That person ended up getting the job! There are countless stories like this, where I have gone out of my way to help someone, knowing that I was going to get nothing in return. Well, that's not completely fair. I did get the reward of helping someone in need, and sometimes that is the greatest gift.

There are many dark places in this world. But what about the places that are not obvious? I live in Orange County, California, one of the richest places in the world. Do you think that these people do not need help? You would be wrong.

Even though I live in beautiful America and in an amazing area, South OC, I am exposed to so much need around me. People are really hurting. Granted, a lot of this need is self-inflicted, but it's still need. Now, on the surface, it seems like everyone in South OC has it all figured out. But once you dive in deep with people, you see a different picture. Look carefully. Though put together, they might need help. They will not always admit it or want to be helped at the time.

There are multiple ways to go about helping people. *"How?"* you ask. My philosophy on how we can help people is in three different areas: financially, emotionally and intellectually, and physically. Now, we all have different strengths and are in different seasons of our life. Some of these ways to help people might feel uncomfortable or not within your means. I challenge you to find what is best for you in your life right now. Before assisting anyone financially, make sure your finances are in order. Some people have money to help other people financially. That is the obvious way that most people ask for help. It is worth mentioning that this is not the only way to help people.

Another way to help people is emotionally and intellectually. Some people just need someone to talk to them. Or just need someone to listen to them. It does not always have to involve words. People just need an ear sometimes. If you see someone having a rough day, be a friend and lend an ear. Care for them by just listening. Most people having a difficult time just need a sounding board, someone who cares enough to simply listen. It helps most people process an issue when they can hear it vocalized out loud to another person. On the side, you can always get intellectual and offer advice. Use your technical skills to provide knowledge to assist those who want to learn. Help them grow as individuals. This can be in a one-on-one mentoring scenario or involve a large group. It will look different for each person. But pour your knowledge into people. You possess knowledge that could dramatically impact someone's life.

I saved the best for last (I also do that when I eat). I personally love to get physical when serving. I love putting my body in motion and working hard. I am a physical kind of guy. I love to serve with my hands and feet. I love the other ways to serve too, but I especially love building things, cleaning things—you name it. If it involves my body getting into motion, I love doing it.

Over the years I have served with multiple nonprofits. That is an easy way to get involved in helping people. Most nonprofits have a volunteer program, along with financial needs. Look up your local nonprofits and discover which ones you want to serve. Nonprofits have a great need, so any help you provide will be appreciated. You can also take a proactive role and create your own ways to get involved in the community.

I am a creative person, who likes to think outside the box. That is why I came up with a few different ways that—using my philosophy of serving financially, emotionally and intellectually, and physically—I can contribute. Initially I took that "serve philosophy" and created a personal outreach plan with multiple programs that would hopefully attract people to get involved with me. There is power in numbers. One person can make an impact, but a hundred people can make an even greater impact. I created four main programs: Selfless Sunday, Serve Saturday, Community Outreach, and Nonprofit Donations. Let me give you a brief explanation and breakdown of each program.

When I created these programs, I integrated them into my life. Then I realized I could reach more people if I integrated these programs into my company, Barrena Real Estate Group, aka, BREG. These programs basically express my DNA philosophy of serving. I believe it is important when creating a company to create a DNA that resembles its creator, the founder of the company. Just one of my personal philosophies when creating a business. Anyway, I implemented these programs into my company structure. I always like to say that my company is a for-profit company, but we go about our business as a nonprofit. Always looking to serve our community and beyond.

Selfless Sunday is a bi-monthly outreach event sponsored by BREG. This event is very special to me. It is designed as an opportunity to give back to those in our community in desperate need. Think of it as a fundraiser for individuals, families, or groups who long for financial assistance. We give back in two different ways. One: we select a candidate in our community who is in desperate need of financial assistance. Two: we select a local small business to support by promoting and holding an event to raise funds for it. It was designed to be a creative way to give back to individuals truly in need and support local small businesses that are also in need. This would be a way you could financially support those in need.

Serve Saturday is another bi-monthly outreach event sponsored by BREG. This day is designed to be a hands-and-feet volunteer opportunity. I always tell everyone who participates to come ready with a good attitude to get dirty and work hard. Basically, we find local nonprofits that need volunteers. We basically come in and give whatever help they need as long as it is physical in nature. This is how we physically get involved in serving people.

Community Social is a monthly outreach event that BREG sponsors. This special event has two main goals. One: it supports local small business, which I believe is the backbone of economies. Two: it facilitates an environment to "meet and greet" your neighbors in a casual, comfortable setting. We provide beverages and appetizers. And we tell everyone that all are welcome. This would be a way to lend emotional and intellectual help.

Nonprofit Donation is a partnership between BREG and Miracles for Kids. BREG donates a percentage of all our gross revenue to this nonprofit. As I've previously mentioned, it's a beautiful nonprofit that I have grown quite fond of over the years. It truly has a heart to help children and their families who are in desperate, dire need. It truly helps make miracles. This is another way to financially support worthy causes.

I have other nonprofits I regularly donate to. I believe in their mission. It comes down to what I am passionate about, and that is people. People who have real needs. These are the ones I want to see supported. I am thankful for the nonprofits that I have found over the years, which have given me a deep perspective on what is really valuable in life. That is, giving back to those I feel called to financially support.

As you can see, this was a creative way for me to integrate my serving philosophy into my company. And more importantly, my life. Creating a blueprint to be selfless will help cultivate that selflessness.

It does not have to look so strategic on your part. For me, being true to my authentic self, I like to create strategies and plans to execute the mission I have. I am a strategist, though. I do not think a strategy is always necessary. Sometimes it is good enough to just deny yourself, find the need, and get to work.

Just remember that all around the world, in every part of the globe, there are people in need. These people will not get the desperate help they need unless we show up to serve. By serving, you will leave a legacy that will impact generations to come. You will send a ripple effect through the ages that will not be forgotten: not by God or by the people you impact. Lead with love and serve with a purpose, for this is a part of your calling to be your authentic self.

Growth

The lifelong process of education, application, and development

> Intellectual growth should commence at birth and cease only at death.
>
> —*Albert Einstein*

I am not sure how I even graduated from each class in grade school, I cared so little about studying in my early life. For that reason, teachers did not have much patience for me. I was told by numerous educators that I had the abilities but did not have the focus to gain those abilities. Even when I was young, I knew that I was capable, but I did not care about my studies or learning what they wanted to teach me. I only cared to hang out with my friends and have fun. Obviously, there was a deeper issue than just my lack of focus.

As I already mentioned earlier in this book, my father did not set the best example. I cannot recall either of my parents putting much emphasis on the importance of school. Especially as a young man looking at my dad, who was always trying to be the life of the party, I wanted to be like him. He was my main role model. My mother, whom I loved dearly and did look up to, did her best, but the relationship I always craved was one with my dad. Since my mother was always there for me, I took that relationship for granted. It was the father-son bond that I so desperately yearned for. My dad never helped me with homework or anything else related to school. It's not my dad's fault: I take ownership. But nevertheless, the poor example did not help my attitude towards schooling in general.

I used to drive all my teachers absolutely crazy. In some cases, they would blow a gasket and have an outburst at me in class. It was always when I was being a nuisance. Granted, I was a bit of a class clown, always trying to get the attention of my friends and really anyone I could make laugh in class. I was that one kid causing untold issues for the teacher. It was apparent to me that my teachers did not care to help me. I am sure it took a lot of emotional energy to teach me, as I did not listen. Most teachers did not even attempt it, and the ones who did ended up giving up sooner rather than later.

Let's say that I did not fit into the mold that the system created for education. Even though I did not put in the effort, the system did not work for someone like me. More specifically, the teachers did not work for me. Looking back, I am not sure that no one can be taught anything unless first understanding that the messenger or educator cares for them. Someone who shows love through their patience towards their students. Someone who realizes that not everyone thinks and operates the same way. Some people need to be taught in a different way in order to learn something new. That was me. Someone who thought differently.

I can only recall, before I was eighteen, one teacher who had patience and came across like he cared. A history teacher. What his name was, I no longer remember. But he taught at Laguna Hills High School in Orange County, California. In ninth grade, his was my first class of the day. I used to show up extremely high from smoking marijuana with my friends on route to class. The history teacher did not appreciate me showing up high and late, but I could tell he wanted to help me. He was a nice man, who seemed to have good intentions toward me. He did not get far with me, but I appreciated the effort. And I will never forget him for that kindness.

On the other side, in all of my physical education and kinesthetic classes I would get straight A's. I loved paying attention in those classes. It gave me an opportunity to be physical, which I loved. Interestingly to me, so many of the teachers quite obviously did not have the patience or perseverance to help me. I have been sent to the principal's office too many times to count because the educator did not want to deal with my nonsense. It seemed like a near-daily trip. After-school detention was just another class for me, as I was there practically every day.

Looking back, at a young age it is hard to know the importance of education. Most kids struggle with trying to learn new things. If it does not come easy, most kids will get too frustrated and quit on themselves. In time, as you grow older, you realize something I've harped on: that challenge is necessary for growth. The two go hand in hand. But how many kids realize the lifelong benefits of education? Not many. Most kids, like me, just want to have fun. Unless there is someone of influence in their life showing them a better way, they will not know better. I wish I'd had someone like that in my life, but I was not so fortunate. I had to learn the hard way. I am thankful that I had the opportunity to learn at all, as I eventually did learn the importance of challenging myself to learn new things. Growth is necessary not only while in school but also for the rest of our lives.

We are all designed differently. We all learn differently. We all experience growth differently. There are those who lean towards intellectual growth. There are those who lean towards physical growth. We all gravitate towards what is easier for us. The true obstacle is growing in a way that challenges us. *The hard way, not the easy way, is the better way.* Since we all have different desires and skills, it's important to note that we need to focus on both the easy and the hard. One thing that is certain: growth does not come naturally in all areas for each person. It requires a level of work ethic, perseverance, and diligence to learn something new.

It was not until I decided to change my life on that fateful day—July 15, 2001—that I discovered my love for growth and self-improvement. I lived the first eighteen years of my life not challenging my intellect, as it was too difficult—it required too much effort. When I did decide to move in a new direction, I was entering my senior year of high school. By that time, I recognized I'd done myself a lot of damage by goofing off in class. I decided I wanted to put in the work, graduate, and go to college. That does not seem like much for some people, but for me it was going to be a monumental achievement. I learned very quickly how much effort it was really going to take, a ton.

Coming from behind in my senior year, I met with my guidance counselor, whom I'd never met before—did not even know that role existed. I've told this story in Chapter 1—Foundation. When she discouraged me from continuing forward at that high school, saying I would need to be held back one year, I asked her, supposing there *was* a way to graduate on time, what would I have to do? "Enroll in an accelerated, at-home program," she told me, if you remember. So I made the choice to leave my friends and get to work on my studies. That is exactly what I did.

I got focused and learned very quickly that not only was I behind on paper, I was also intellectually behind. I knew I was smart, but at that time I struggled with my intelligence. I put a focus my entire life on sports, hanging out with friends and just having fun. I found it very difficult to learn all of these new things that I paid no attention to, growing up. I only had very basic English and grammar skills, achieved a below-grade-level math level, and all my other skills were poor at best. Since I was so behind in my studies, and multiple educators had told me I had ADD (attention deficit disorder), I was really shaky at the beginning. Not to mention that everything I was learning was boring and unimportant to me. I had no passion or excitement behind my studies.

I kept thinking thoughts that were not my own. Thoughts like *I am not smart enough, I will never be smart enough, I'm too far behind to catch up, I'm not capable, I'm not good enough, I cannot focus.* And finally, *I am out right stupid.* These thoughts were in my mind on a loop like a constantly repeating movie. To be honest, I did not even believe them, but they were still there. That is why I say they were not from me. Personally, I believe there are three forces that invade our minds: good forces from God's dominion, evil forces from Satan's dominion, and our personal consciousness (which is all of our past experiences and education).

You might not be aware that this is actually a biblical principle. It is quite apparent to me, based on my life and the lives of those around me, that there are forces outside of us guiding and directing us. At the end of the day, it is our choice to choose our own path, but these forces are still there. They are all around us, whether we see them or not. They are invisible forces—which I know sounds crazy. But read in between the lines and you will see what I am seeing. We are in a battle. That battle is against our mind and heart.

There is a book in the Bible that is nearly 2000 years old called Ephesians. The author makes a profound statement: "For our struggle is not against flesh and blood, but against the rulers, against the powers, against the world forces of this darkness, against the spiritual forces of evil in the heavenly realms." I get it; this might sound crazy to you but look around you. Isn't it evident in our lives? Just simply look at the division amongst people in this world. More importantly, just look at the war that wages in your own mind.

No one, and I mean no one, is in a continual state of bliss and peace. If they are, they are either lying to themselves or ignoring the truth. We are all in this spiritual battle together. This battle is physically unseen but real. God's goodness and demons' evilness do exist. There is a battle between good and evil. *What's on the line?*

you ask. Your souls. The battle is against our minds and hearts. The ultimate victor in this battle has already been announced, yet there are still many smaller battles to come. The winner of those battles is looking to conquer your soul for all eternity.

I say all this to make you aware of what is already going on all around us. Realize that your thoughts are not always your own. The good news is you are not alone in this battle. You can be on the winning side. It is not too late to make the right choice. As always, the choice is yours. God has given us all that gift. Choose Christ, as He is the ultimate victor of your soul. He paid the ultimate price, coming down from His throne above to sacrifice Himself as the once-and-for-all atonement of our wrongdoings. He loved us before we even knew Him. He loves us, even if we have cursed Him. He is faithful and He is good. He cares for you. He cares for me.

Simply surrender your life to Jesus. He is faithful to forgive your past mistakes and create a new heart and mind in you. He only asks that you give Him everything, as He has given you everything. He wants all of you, and not 1 percent less. Choose Him, and you will not be disappointed. His word and promise do not return voided. I know this to be true. He has been faithful and good to me. He has never abandoned or disappointed me. I have been a follower of Jesus for twenty-two years now. I should not have made it this far, but this is why I did. That is why He gets my everything. The choice is yours, no pressure from me. I only care enough to share my heart.

So, inevitably, I conquered the battle in my mind. I joined an accelerated program where I was able to make up practically an additional year within my senior year of high school. I even ended up graduating a few months early. It took hard work. It was a great accomplishment, but I was already focused on the next milestone, where to go to college. I did not know what I wanted to academically specialize in.

As I've already recounted, I ended up getting accepted to a college called "Joshua Wilderness Institute" up in a small town called

"Hume Lake" in California, up near Yosemite National Forest. It was also an accelerated program. It was a Christian-based college that condensed a four-year program into one year. Sounds a little far-fetched, right? Well, the program was quite vigorous. Some might even call it militant. Which, honestly, was perfect for me. I always considered myself to thrive in challenging environments. I love the fight, love the grind, since I am willing to put in the work and feel the ultimate pain of this habit growth.

Joshua was a co-ed program that pretty much split down the middle between women and men. We had fewer than a hundred students in total. The application process was quite vigorous and competitive. I have heard the program is even more competitive now. When I applied, I was told that for the one hundred spots available, several thousand applied. So, it was extremely competitive. The director said he only wanted to see the students who were ready for the journey ahead and who were 100 percent committed to becoming their best leader. My director's name was Darren McWatters. He was one of only two men I have ever looked up to as a spiritual leader. The other person is Dr. Daniel Nehrbass, who is a good friend and mentor who also had an extremely big impact on my life. I am grateful for both these men.

Once you were accepted into Joshua's program, you had to sign a contract that would last the full year's program. This contract had many commitments, but three really stood out. Rule number one: no media whatsoever. Mind you, this was 2002. Obviously, a very different time compared to now. Nevertheless, we were not allowed to have computer or phone access and could not listen to music on any devices or watch television or anything else that gave us the escape to unplug from the program.

Joshua demanded that you had your full attention at all times on their program. Rule number two: the opposite sex "odd and even rule." You were not allowed to be alone with the opposite sex. No one in the program was married, but some left relationships back home.

Even if you took a trip back home to see your love interest, you two were not allowed to be alone together. If there was someone of the opposite sex in the room, you had to have another person there, whether of the same sex or opposite. Again, Joshua demanded your full attention on the program, and dating served as another potential distraction.

Rule number three: you had only two days off every month. During those two days you could go back home or stay in town.

I had fourteen-to-eighteen-hour days scheduled every day all that next year. Those two days off a month, I—and everyone else—coveted. You were so tired that you basically took that time to sleep. Mind you, you had no access to media, so the only turn-off outlet was sleep.

This was militant. It was an extremely vigorous program. I thrived in that environment, literally; that program was built for people like me. There were other little rules—no drinking, smoking, drugs, and a bunch of other taboo things—but most everyone who went into the program did not have problems with them. What bothered us were the items we were accustomed to that all of a sudden were taken away.

This college was leadership focused. The primary goal was to immerse the students in a program that would create a strong leader. If you could not hack it, you would be excused with no refund. The program was not cheap; it cost a pretty penny.

We were challenged in pretty much every direction. Monday through Friday, we had to wake up at 6:00 a.m. to start our day, spending an hour with God. This time with God could be spent praying, journaling, meditating, or reading God's word, aka., the Bible. During this time you were not allowed to be in your dorm room but had to be somewhere on campus, in the library or somewhere else. If you were caught sleeping or failed to use your time, you faced disciplinary actions. At Joshua, those disciplinary actions were not just for you but for the entire class. No exceptions. If someone made a mistake at Joshua, everyone paid the price.

You can imagine the effect this had. For instance, once some students were caught sleeping during their time with God in the morning. The director announced to all of us during breakfast that everyone had a special assignment for the day. We did not know what it was, but we did know that all the students were going to be punished for the mistakes of a few. That is the way it worked at Joshua. The director had us all meet around 7:00 a.m. sharp at a construction yard in town.

The yard was full of everything you could imagine, from broken, abandoned vehicles to miscellaneous heavy machinery like tractors and trailers. At this point we were all very curious as to what we were going to do. Well, the assignment was simple. We were to be divided up into three groups. Each group was to be given a specific task which was to carry rocks from one spot to another spot. Group A was in charge of picking up pebble-like rocks that were 1-to-5 pounds each. We were allowed to use our hands, shirts, or whatever else we could find in the yard to help. We carried them all the way down this hill, which was roughly a hundred yards away. Group B was in charge of picking up rocks that took two hands, between 15 and 50 pounds each. That group had to carry the rocks about fifty yards across the construction yard. The last group, Group C, was in charge of rolling or dragging these 100-to-300-pound rocks about twenty yards. We did find some rope. That helped.

Beyond the task, we were told there were two separate rules. Rule 1, no talking whatsoever. Everyone had to be devoted to silence. Rule 2, every hour, each group would change tasks. Group A would take on group B's task; group B would then do group C's task; it went on in that rotation until we finished. That's the other thing; there were so many rocks it was not possible to be finished in a day, yet the punishment was for the day. At least, so we thought. So, we were doing a task with no end in sight. That made it pretty hard for some people. Personally, I absolutely loved it! I love anything physical and enjoyed the break from regular studies. Not many had my attitude. Some students were quite perturbed since they felt they had not made a mistake, and so, why were they being punished?

After laboring all morning, we were told we were allowed to go up for lunch and we could talk during lunch. You'll love this part . . . At the end of lunch, which was an hour, the director told us we were to head back down, as we were going to do the same thing, yet with a twist. We were to move all of the rocks back to where we originally found them. When we finished this task, our punishment was over. I loved the reaction from everyone! People were *not* pleased. I myself was laughing inside. So, we all went back down and put the rocks back. By the time we finished and headed back up to the college, dusk had fallen. It was around 7:00 p.m. So, it was a twelve-hour disciplinary action. No student ever made the mistake of falling asleep during quiet time again.

Back to Joshua's normal routine. After sixty minutes with God's word, we had another sixty minutes to eat breakfast and get ready for the day. Classes began at 8:00 a.m. sharp. We had three classes (an hour and a half to two hours long) each day. These classes had fantastic professors. The topics included theology, consequences of ideas, other religions, leadership training, philosophy, and more.

Another good way to look at Joshua—it was a think-tank for your life. It was a year set aside to focus, every minute, on the details of each of our lives. To truly understand who we were so that we could understand who we could become as leaders. An assignment in one of the classes was to memorize an entire book of the Bible, Philippians. We had to memorize it word for word in the NIV translation. We had to be able to audibly repeat it and kinesthetically write it on paper. We memorized all 1,629 words. That was a pretty cool experience, especially for someone like me, who did not intellectually challenge himself until later in life. I was not sure of my memorizing capabilities since I had never challenged that part of my brain. It took work, but it's an accomplishment I will never forget. I was grateful for the challenge.

We had two classes in the morning before lunch. Then the third and final class right after lunch. After that, we had a couple hours to ourselves to study, do our daily chores, or do whatever else suited us. That is right, every day each student had the responsibility for a chore. We had a chore board. Chores could be vacuuming the library and community room or cleaning the public restrooms or helping cook for breakfast, lunch, or dinner, and many other miscellaneous tasks. If we did not complete these daily tasks, as just recounted, the whole group was punished with more chores. Personally, I loved it when we got punished. I am truly a glutton for punishment. But that is a separate thought that we can talk about later.

After our free time, we had dinner, followed by nightly leadership training for a couple hours. I thoroughly enjoyed that. Every week the school would invite speakers to give us a training for the week. These speakers were incredible! Renowned authors, professors, pastors, leaders, and many other influential people. Honestly, some of the speakers were life changing for all of us. Absolutely mind-blowing!

We spent our Friday night through Sunday evening working in town. Each week we were assigned a new job. Hume Lake, as I've mentioned earlier, is a small mountain town that only had a couple hundred residents aside from the Joshua program. The town was so small that there was one café, one general store, and one gas station. You get it: it was extremely tiny. We did, however, have a pool table, basketball court, ice skating rink, and huge lake. Those were pretty much all the amenities. So weekends, we students would work somewhere in town. Unless of course we had our two days off for the month, in which case we were free to do whatever we wanted. I really enjoyed the weekend. On Friday nights we only had to work a few hours, but on Saturday and Sunday it was a normal eight-or-so-hour shift.

As a side note, I enjoyed working in town so much that at the conclusion of the Joshua program, the Ponderosa Banquet Hall offered me a full-time job. In the end, I took the job, staying for a whole additional year. I ended up living in Hume Lake for two years. I loved it! I knew it was not going to be a forever job for me, but I thoroughly enjoyed the environment and the overall learning experience.

At Joshua, roughly every month we went on a different mission trip. The mission trips usually lasted about a week. We did a lot of missions—on one of which we learned sign language for a couple months. Then we went to a deaf orphanage in Mexico for about ten days to love on the kids and help where needed. We also went to Texas for a Billy Graham Crusade. If you do not know the name "Billy Graham," he was an extremely impactful individual. He devoted over eight decades to preaching the name of Jesus, with, according to Wikipedia, an "estimated lifetime audience, including radio and television broadcasts, that topped billions of people." He traveled the world, changing lives, including having desegregated audiences and befriending Martin Luther King. He also preached with Johnny Cash. Extremely influential and selfless, he devoted his life to other people.

Billy Graham events brought hundreds of thousands of people from all around the world to come listen. We had the opportunity at the Dallas Cowboys' AT&T Stadium in Texas to assist in any way the staff needed. People had to park so far away that we were in charge of picking people up who could not walk efficiently or were in wheelchairs and bringing them about a mile back and forth to the stadium. It was a pretty cool experience. On another trip we got to go serve the homeless in Los Angeles. The primary objective of this trip was to teach people about the love of Jesus. Basically, we told people about Jesus as the Savior of the world. We not only got to talk to people on the streets, but we also got to evangelize to the inmates in a local prison.

All of those trips were life changing. It gives you a different perspective on life when you can travel around our nation and the world to see how people live and function. I have always had a passion for people. Of course, I want people to know about Jesus and what He has done for me, but I love to just love on people. I know what it is like to feel broken, abandoned, and alone. I know those life circumstances are necessary for growth, but I do not want anyone to experience that pain alone. The pain I experienced in my life drives me to help those who want the help.

After that year in Joshua's program, I reflected on all I had accomplished. It was an incredible year, filled with incredible experiences and memories. I was able to see myself be challenged and come up on top. Joshua's program was also designed to allow the students to take a Sabbath. This time was to reflect on who you are in Christ as a leader and child of God. To challenge yourself to step up to be your best leader. You might be familiar with that term "Sabbath" or not. Sabbath is time you set aside to be at rest with God. It is that simple. I was fortunate enough to take off an entire year as my Sabbath season. I learned so much in that year that I carry with me today.

At Joshua, it was driven home to me, the importance of being a lifelong student. When I first thought about going to college, I was under the impression that I was going to learn something I would then apply to a career, and that was going to be the end of my education. Not at all. Just like Albert Einstein said, "Intellectual growth should commence at birth and cease *only* at death." I have never wanted to be average; *I have always wanted to be the best that I can be.* I realized that I need to constantly challenge my mind just the way I challenged my body. It took a lot of work in mental development to learn how to focus and absorb new learning. I am not going to lie; it has been extremely difficult over the years. But I had to learn how to push through adversity.

After college I went down a path of constant learning. I opened my mind to always being a student. Going to numerous other colleges, I then discovered my calling as an entrepreneur. Since I finished college (I went to four colleges total), I have completed well over thirty programs in self-development, real estate, mortgage, financing, property management, exercise science, corrective exercise, sports performance, entrepreneurship, business strategy, digital marketing, real-estate law, and the list goes on and on and on. On these topics I have read hundreds of books. I typically read or listen to one to four books a month. I have done that for decades. I do not care to mention all of the national certifications, licenses, and credentials. Those do not mean anything to me other than a track record of my constant growth as a lifelong student.

I am only forty years old. Hopefully, God willing, I have at least another sixty years left of educating myself. I am so excited about all the new things I will learn about myself, others, and life in general. It gets me all giddy inside to think about all the new things I am going to discover. I can hardly wait. I plan to be patient, put in the work, and continue to learn as much as I can about whatever I can.

Out of all the things I have learned over the years, there is one daily routine I have that is the real culprit of my success as a student. I spend time with God every day. I get in His word, I talk with Him, write in a journal about Him, and simply have a relationship with Him. He is my significance. He is my reason to have reason in the first place. He is my beginning and end. Without Him guiding me and directing me, I am a nobody. I am only as good as the One who saved me. I am a nobody, just trying to preach about somebody and this somebody is Jesus Christ the Savior of the world. I am sure there are plenty of people who disagree with me. I am OK with that. But, in order for me to be my authentic self, I have to keep it real with you. I am nobody without Him.

My encouragement for you is to never stop learning. To be a lifelong student is to be in a constant state of growth. That growth will lead you down a path of discovering your authentic self. If you are like I was, and believe you are not smart enough or intellectually capable, I am telling you, that is a lie from pure evilness. You are good enough. God designed you exactly as He wanted to design you. You are perfectly created in God's image. There are no flaws in God's design. There are no mistakes.

If you have a handicap in your intellect, then break through that barrier. *How?* you ask. Stop making excuses and do whatever it takes. Put in the effort to give your 100 percent in everything you do. Do not sell yourself short. You have greatness inside. You might have to work harder than you have ever worked to get it out. If you put in the work, you will get the results. Remember, anything in life worth doing is going to take significant effort. Do not let anyone tell you otherwise. Know your worth, understand your gifts, and be diligent to learn new things.

My proposition to you is to take a Sabbath and confront your thoughts. It is your choice how often you will do this. Weekly? Monthly? Quarterly? The point is, you decide. You are the boss of you! Take time to spend with yourself and God, alone, away from distractions. Maybe you do not believe in God. Well, spend time with yourself in nature, enjoying creation. That time with yourself will allow you to reflect on what you want in this life and who you want to be. *Take time to challenge your thoughts. Test them. Ask real questions to yourself that make you doubt everything.* Go on. Try it. It will make you all the more grounded in what you believe. When you are grounded in knowing who you are, you will have the conviction to stand up for what you believe in.

Just know that this process of taking time for yourself, challenging yourself, and learning new things is a forever process. Be patient. Once you stop learning, you stop growing. When you stop growing, you are only dying inside. Do not kill your growth but thrive in challenging your intellect on a regular basis. Pick up a good book, join a course or program, learn something that challenges you.

Do not think inside the box but think outside the box. Be a critical thinker. Think for yourself and not what others have told you to think. Be a lifelong student. Never give up on your intellect. You are worth it.

Discipline

Someone who maintains faithful consistency in their commitments

> Therefore I run in such a way, as not without aim; I box in such a way, as not beating the air; but I discipline my body and make it my slave.
>
> —*The Apostle Paul*

From the outside, looking in, someone might think I have always been disciplined. Truth told, the first eighteen years of my life I lived quite undisciplined. My life was quite chaotic, unorganized. I was the opposite of a disciplined person. I did not follow through on my commitments. I lived quite selfishly. It was all about me. Living a disciplined life requires diligence, perseverance, and vision. It is difficult to follow through on your commitments unless you push past the pain and see a brighter future. Discipline is not for the faint of heart but for those who want more out of life than just to exist and go through the daily motions.

In my former life, I coasted—through everything. No real effort and discipline was present. I just existed, with a sense of living day-by-day and never really focusing on the future. I had discipline in minor ways, such as skateboarding, as you know. But anytime there was resistance with getting to the next level, I would give up. If it did not come naturally, then it required too much effort. I saw some of those people in my life who had the discipline to push through the challenging growth seasons that helped them to reach their goals. That was not me, though. If it was too hard. I would give up fairly quickly.

I am surprised and humbled that I even made it through that time in my life. Back then I was just downright sloppy. That is why I am so passionate about the importance of discipline in my life now. If it was not for the first eighteen years, I would not appreciate what it takes to be disciplined. Not many people live a life of discipline; rather, they live with a sense of leisure towards their dreams and ambitions. Most people give up on their dreams at a young age. In most cultures dreaming is seen as something for kids and not adults. But I say to adults it first begins with dreaming. Dream first to achieve your goals later. Then still dream big and know you can accomplish almost anything you set your mind to.

Though I want to give the majority of the credit to my God, who pulled me out of the trenches and into a marvelous life with Him, I also have to give a lot of credit to my mom; she was so adamant about how I could accomplish anything I set my mind to. I still hear those words Mom ingrained in my mind. Thank you, Mom, for always believing in me. You could say that it is a parent's job to believe in her children and encourage them. But my mom took it to a whole 'nother level.

All the while I knew I was not giving my best effort, my mom was telling me that I was capable so long as I was willing to commit and be disciplined to put in the effort. In my mind, I had a fallback plan. I knew that I was not trying in life but that when I was ready to commit to something, there was nothing standing in my way. The only thing standing in my way was myself. I am human like anyone else. When I felt pain and discomfort, I wanted to run in the other direction. No one likes experiencing discomfort unless they train their mind otherwise.

It was not until July 15, 2001, that I decided to be a disciplined man. I told myself that I would follow through with my commitments. I was given a second chance at life. No one, and I mean no one, was going to stop me from living my best life. Back then, God spoke to me clearly. He told me that I would do great things and accomplish much in this life but only alongside Him. I believed it back then, and I believe it now. God is so faithful to pursue us when we do not pursue Him. If it weren't for His relentless love, I would not be where I am.

When looking back on the last two decades, I see a track record of consistency. A disciplined life. A life of purpose, of passion. When you think about it, those things that come easy will probably be forgotten, anyway. It is through the challenging circumstances of our lives that we reach heights we will never forget.

I can think of countless things I have accomplished in the last twenty-two years—not one of which did not require discipline. When I went to college up at Joshua, I needed the discipline and vision to get me through the program. Not just get through but grow. All of the accomplishments while at Joshua allowed me to grow and understand that to accomplish anything, discipline is a mandatory trait. When memorizing the book of Philippians, I really had to wrap my mind around doing something never on my radar to accomplish. *Memorizing an entire book? What in the world?* I thought to myself. OK, it's only just over three Biblical pages, with small print. I only achieved that goal through daily effort, persistence, and discipline.

There are certain people who can perform a task like memorizing a book easier than others. We all have learning disabilities, or distinctions. Ways we learn. Some people have mental handicaps that confront them, as I did; for others, it's physical handicaps. No one is extraordinarily good at everything. Some things in this life are going to stretch us so much we want to quit. For me, memorizing the book of Philippians was one of my greater challenges. I can say in the end I did memorize the entire text word for word. That, undoubtedly, was an accomplishment for me.

When I met the love of my life, we were both young. We were full of passion for each other. To be quite honest, it caught us both off guard. We were both disinterested in finding that someone. Both focused on life. That is why it was meant to be. Meeting each other was surreal. Feelings developed so fast. I remember asking my mom a question right at the outset. I asked my mom if it was possible to love someone only after a couple of weeks. My mom gave me a simple and profound answer. She said, "Yes, I believe you can. Love is a commitment and a feeling. Typically, they both do not arrive at the same time. Either the commitment comes first, and the feelings follow, or the feelings are there first and the commitment comes."

After my mom told me that, I knew I loved my wife-to-be. In a mere three weeks I told her. She reciprocated, as I've mentioned earlier, but the unfolding, the cementing, took time. Maybe not that much time, but it did take some time. My mom was right. The feelings we had in the beginning opened the door to a beautiful life. But it has been the commitment that has made us get this far. Now, you might think love was enough, and all would be smooth from then on. But marriage—any marriage, no matter how beautiful—is also extremely difficult at times. You are faced with two different personalities, past experiences, and individuals who do not always see eye to eye. It takes commitment to never lose sight of how much you love each other on a regular basis.

Prior to changing my life, I never planned to marry. I was like most men. To be transparent, I was horny. I really just wanted to have sex with a ton of women and enjoy a casual sex life. Thankfully, I did not take that path, as I see how unfulfilling it would have wound up being. God had other plans for me. I thought His plans were better, so I switched paths. Food for thought: my wife and I did not have sex before we got married. From the time we met to the day we got married, thirty-two sometimes excruciatingly long months (on my part), we waited to finally make sweet, passionate love. That took an extreme commitment. Many times, we got quite close. Almost gave in. It was not easy at all, but we wanted to wait. That was important to us.

Just afterwards, I picked up the game of golf. I was twenty-five. I was a newlywed. I got the golf bug. If you are a golfer, you understand that fever. I undertook a sport I had no business playing. Why? I was a bodybuilder. *Bodybuilders do not play golf.*

I had earlier started lifting weights. I was around 147 pounds soaking wet. I was also a marathon runner. I decided I wanted to put on some muscle. I got really involved in lifting weights and dieting correctly. In just a matter of a few years, I shot all the way up to 227 pounds at my peak weight. I did put on a little bit of fat, but it was primarily muscle. Being 80 pounds heavier than my natural weight did not work for golf.

Needless to say, I decided I wanted to get good at golf. I committed to practicing every day for at least a short time. I also had to slim down. So I weighed in at a very lean 185. Just a short eleven months from when I started playing, I shot my first under-par round. If you are not familiar with golf, anything at par or under is considered to be at a scratch, or professional, level. Just a scant year after that, I was more consistent at scoring low. So, as you know, I decided to go professional, competing in a lot of small golf tour events up and down California.

Golf was not built for my body, *but I got good at it by adapting to a new blueprint* and committing to getting better. Without that blueprint, that discipline and drive, I would have never been able to play at that level, much less enroll, as I've described elsewhere, in Q-School, in order to qualify to go on the PGA tour, the most elite golf tour in the world, where all the best professionals compete. That never came to fruition. I realized I was good but not good enough. So, I decided to get good at something else, business.

Even though I had been an entrepreneur and business owner for nearly a decade, it was not until 2015 that I decided to hang up my golf clubs. At the time I was a personal trainer, owned a gym, had an online company, and I was studying to get my real-estate license. I was ambitious. I had a ton of motivation. I wanted to change the world, and my wife and I were planning on getting pregnant with our first child. That really motivated me to make the money that was necessary. I was always the breadwinner at home, and adding an additional life motivated me to another level.

After deciding to put in the work in my businesses, I grew my personal-training business by 30 percent, my online business about 150 percent, and obtained my real-estate license. My first year in real estate was quite difficult. I was this already-successful entrepreneur, stepping into a completely different industry. Being in the fitness industry is casual in dress code but also serious on the business side. It is a very fun-loving, motivating industry. The real-estate world is totally different: very serious about the dress code and even more serious on the business side. It is not a fun-loving, motivating industry. It was quite clear to me that it was all about making money through selling real estate. Oh, yeah, and to help clients too. At least, this was the attitude I saw when first getting into the industry.

To be honest, I really struggled with it. I initially hung my license at an office that did not mesh well with my personality. I ended up going to a different office. In real-estate sales when you get your license, you are considered an independent contractor, or business owner. That agent has to hang their license under a real-estate broker. You cannot do real-estate sales unless you hang your license under a licensed broker. Well, after switching offices and putting in the work for nearly a year, I was able to accomplish my income goal. That goal was simple. If I got into real estate, I wanted to make an extra $100,000 a year. Well, after that first year I made $23,000 and I really thought twice about doing real-estate sales.

That first year I worked the hardest, doing numerous hours of cold calling, door knocking, contacting my network, and pitching leads. Not much paid off. I was patient. I knew my hard work was going to reap returns in due time. Well, it did, as the second year I was able to easily exceed my income goal, which I have been able to do every year since. Were it not for my determination to see my commitment through, I would have absolutely given up. Discipline was my driving force. I had to push through the bleak, unclear initial season, when I could not see the light at the end of the tunnel, to make it to where I am today. No wonder tons of people give up on real estate after getting their license; it is not easy. It takes hard work to be successful in this industry.

I wanted to be a dad so badly. If I was to have multiple kids (which I was hoping for) I specifically wanted a little girl first. I thought it was a cool idea to have a tough little girl, aka, a woman who would grow up to take this world by storm. Who I would also call my little princess warrior. I loved the idea of helping raise a strong woman who would be a leader to impact the world for good.

My little tough girl, my princess warrior, would grow into a woman who would not settle for mediocrity. Well, after years of waiting and nearly a decade of being married, we ended up having our little girl when I was thirty-three. I waited what seemed like an eternity for that little girl. Then we ended up having a beautiful boy, who is my number-one guy. We are best buds for life. If you don't know by now, my kids are my world. They are so incredibly special. I always dreamed of being the best dad I could be. When that moment of fatherhood finally arrived, I was over the moon with joy. Words could not come close to describing my happiness.

I realized quite quickly: *This is not easy*. Not only is it challenging to develop the sort of relationship you want with your kids, but it is also potentially a strain on the marriage. It is easy to make it about the kids, and no longer about your significant other. That is not an option for me. My wife is my best friend and my bride forever. I am committed to her for always and forever. I do not always succeed at this, but she is my earthly number one. I want to make her my priority, and then I want to be the best parent I can be for my children. My goal is not only to be an outstanding father but a mentor who guides them and a friend who supports them.

As a parent I have had to work on myself to be my best for them. My kids are only four and six, so I am still in the thick of it. This mission is not accomplished yet. Not only am I investing in growing my mind through reading books and listening to podcasts to be the best parent I can be but spending the much-needed time that my kids and I so desperately crave. As mentioned, I take my kids at least once a week on an individual date. They love this time and of course, I do too. I try to spend as much family time as I can with them. I can do better at this one.

To be fully transparent, in some ways this habit—being disciplined—is hard for me. I have ambitions to change millions of lives around the world. Yet, I want to excel in parenting; I want to be the best husband I can be. It is a constant balancing act. I can tell you, as I go through the thick of this season, I am still in the process of learning. I will not give up. I will come back to this topic at the end of the book.

Currently, I am in an interesting season. As I have stated before, I am a real-estate broker and owner of a company called Barrena Real Estate Group. Since I decided in January 2023 just to focus on my real-estate business, my company has grown tremendously. I signed up a new team member the other day, and now we are up to twenty-one. I love my team. They are exceptional people. I can go on about each of them, but just know that I am privileged to work with them. We have a combination of agents, marketing department, and administrative staff. And I am loving every minute of it.

We are in one of the more difficult seasons in real estate right now. I knew going into this there were going to be some growing pains. So far I have been right. It has also been a blessed year full of joys and many accomplishments. While I have been growing my real-estate company, I decided to start writing this book. I decided there is no time like the present. In my mind, I take extreme ownership of my life. If there is something I want to accomplish, why wait? Let's get it done right now. So, I started writing, and oh what a journey it has been. Love it!

On paper, it made sense to start writing my book. I had a vision for what I wanted to accomplish with it. That vision is a part of a much bigger vision for the many books to come. I do not see myself as a one-time author. I am writing this book with two main goals: to help people and help myself. I am hoping to impact people through this book. Hoping to encourage and teach people a practical method for finding their authentic self. How does one become an authentic, genuine, real person? I've had that discussion too many times to count. It's a broken-record conversation I've had with countless people over the decades. Clearly, in this book, I offer some answers, the fruits of twenty-two years of studies and work on being my authentic self.

On the other hand, I am attempting to define thoughts that are buried in my head. Writing allows me to get my thoughts and feelings on paper, thus, feel real. To paraphrase again my director in college, Darin McWatters said, "It is one thing to think random thoughts, but it is a whole 'nother thing to clearly define them on paper." My translation, thoughts, and ideas are not real until I put them in clear, audible words or on paper. That is what I am trying to do, clearly define my thoughts on paper. I am giving you inside information as to what I am thinking right now. Like literally this very second. Defining these thoughts in words on a page allows me to speak my truth to others, using my book, which is tangible and real. That delights me.

It leaves me feeling excited about the unknown. By unknown, I mean, "What does life look like *after* my book has been published? *Will life be the same or will it be different?* Different *how?*" I believe it will be different in the best of ways. I foresee a new chapter ahead. Life continues to move me in an exhilarating direction. I am just trying to be candid with you and give you some inside information as to what my mind is currently thinking.

Whether through directly impacting a reader of this book or indirectly impacting someone because of it (perhaps you read this book and exert influence on others as a result), the unknown is exciting to me. The yet-to-be. The challenges that lie ahead. The mystery of it all. Does that not thrill you? Stimulate you? It does me! Today I am living in my present authentic state, and tomorrow, who knows what life has to bring? Seriously heady stuff!

Currently, I am receiving an increased number of opportunities to speak in front of large groups. In the past I have spoken to large audiences and felt like I had a natural talent. I always had a desire to do more public speaking. Not because I believe I am the best at it or want to be recognized, in the spotlight; rather, I want to see people realize their authentic self, their best life, and ultimately accomplish their greatest potential in this beautiful life.

Sharing my present-time thoughts about this book and my journey over the years is my way of illustrating what it takes to accomplish something. There is a process to everything. It doesn't just happen overnight. There are many people in this life who will try to drag you down. There are forces at play that look to detour you. The question is, are you going to let those forces stop you? *Those forces could just be you in your own head.* Are you going to let yourself get in your own way? Are you ready to do something about it? Well, if you are ready, there is no time like the present. I always say Carpe NOW because you are only guaranteed this very second.

Personally, I am incredibly grateful for my second chance at living a disciplined life. In my first life my motto was to live each day to the fullest *for myself.* To do what I wanted to do when I wanted to do it. Even if it hurt people in or around my circle, I didn't care. I found my purpose in the present day and could not see past that. As I have been given a second chance at life, in this life, I choose to live a disciplined life. One full of ambition and drive.

Whereas my life used to be full of selfishness, now I am a simple servant of my surroundings—in any and every way I can help people. Simply opening a door for someone or speaking truth into someone's life, it does not matter to me what shape or form I deliver that service in. What matters is that I do serve those around me. It is the complete opposite life, 180 degrees from how I used to live. I am a different person than I used to be. When I decided to change my life, I committed to a better way. I committed to a purpose that was not all about me. It was about serving others in any and every way I can. I have been given this second chance and I will not waste it.

Whether I have one day or a hundred years, I plan to follow through with my commitments. I pledge to give my all to those around me. If you are lost and without direction, you are not alone. This life is ruthless at times. This life does not always play fair. There is no one who is not susceptible to pain and anguish. Some of the pain in your life could be the result of your own personal choices. Let me ask you an honest question, "Are you following through with your commitments?"

Are you the sort of person who follows through with what you say you will do? Or are you like most people? You say one thing and do another. Do you have a goal or dream that you have yet to accomplish? Are you even working towards it? There is no time like right now. You are not guaranteed the future. Are you ready to follow through with your commitments? It really is as simple as doing what you say you will do. I know it is not easy. I am human, just like you. I know failures do not feel good. But I can tell you, having accomplished what I have, it is possible with diligence and discipline.

I only want to see you succeed in life. Yet success will come with hardships.

You might work towards a goal and find resistance. You might need to change your plans up a little bit. Create a new blueprint instead of working off old plans. The point is, do not give up on yourself. Make yourself useful today and focus on the future. Focusing on the future will allow you to be fulfilled in working towards something that is not easy. Do not take the easy way out. Nothing in this life worth doing is easy. There is something I have observed over the years when trying to accomplish anything. I call it "The Great Trade." I have never heard or read about it elsewhere. It is just a simple observation that I have noticed.

In The Great Trade, in order for someone to accomplish anything, that person has to trade one thing for another. The trade is never easy. The trade is always hard. So, the trade is balanced. You want to accomplish something great? You have to do something very difficult. You want to achieve a goal or dream? You have to endure the pain of achieving that goal or dream. You want to be admired? Then you have to be ridiculed. You want to be in a position of power? Then you have to give up your power to another. You want to be first? Then you have to be last. There is no way around "The Great Trade." I am not perfect, so I could be wrong, but I have looked at The Great Trade from every angle. I do not see a way around The Great Trade.

The only thing that resembles a way around The Great Trade is the free gift of God in Jesus Christ. Undeniably, in His word God says this gift is free and cannot be earned (Romans 6:23). "For the wages of sin is death, but the free gift of God is eternal life in Christ Jesus our Lord." Ephesians 2:8 through 9: "For by Grace you have been saved through faith; and that not of yourselves, it is the gift of God; not as a result of works, so that no one may boast." You see, it is 100 percent a free gift.

Though there is nothing you can do to earn salvation, as it is a free gift, there is still a trade. After you receive His free gift, you must lay down your life and commit to Him forever. The life of a Christian is not easy. Yes, there are Christians who go about it in the wrong way and who try to force the gospel down people's throats. But the Christian life is a life devoted to God and loving others. Those who are genuinely trying to help people in any way possible. Yes, Christians want people to know about Jesus, but first and foremost it is about loving those in need. And we are all in some sort of need. Those who live the Christian life outface a ton of persecution. In America it is not so bad. But in other countries you are martyred for your faith as a Christian, no questions asked.

The Christian life is not an easy life at all. We literally have to pick up our cross daily. Picking up our cross is to be ridiculed, judged, thought of as less than, categorized, and even put to death. You see, even accepting God's free gift, there is a Great Trade. The Christian life is not for the faint of heart. To be a Christian is to be a Christ follower. Not just a believer in Jesus but a devout daily follower. One who lives a life of sacrifice and discipline. One who does not choose the easy way out but the hard way. To live a life of possible punishment and ridicule. To me, this is the life I want to live. I stand for what I believe in. If you do not like it, it is OK with me. Can it not be OK with you? I hope I will always choose the right choice—to love and assist those who do not love and assist me. I do not serve to be served but to help others with no strings attached. Now, that is a hard life. Loving people who despise and hate you. Only God can grant such love. That is my view, at least.

So you see, The Great Trade is absolutely necessary. If you are looking to achieve new heights, then you have to trade one thing for another. There are certain things that might be deal breakers for you. This trade might be one of them. It is good to be aware of this Great Trade. I have deal breakers. One of which is my faith in Christ. The other is my family. I have other deal breakers, but these are the most pronounced in my mind. You have to decide in your mind what you are willing to trade for your success. If you are not willing to trade, then you must be willing to not achieve that goal.

Once you have decided what you are willing to trade and you have committed to follow through until you reach that goal, you are ready to take ownership of your life. Taking ownership means that you can no longer blame anyone else for your shortcomings or disadvantages. The ball is in your court; you are the only person to blame. You are the only person on the field who is in charge of making the plays. Those who take ownership of their life do not make excuses. They do not moan about their lack of time or resources. They make it happen. And if they cannot figure out how, they look for someone who can help them make it happen.

Two individuals who come to mind that portray this sort of mentality are dear friends of mine: Jared and Megan Carver. Starting with a simple thought, Jared created a marketing company called Millennial Media Group, and Megan oversees all its operations. I have seen the company grow to become the highly successful branding company it is today through that never-quit attitude. They took extreme ownership—doing their best—to grow their company. I have seen them work as a team, demonstrating their resolve to be the best, knowing they can do it because of their discipline. That discipline led them to a high rate of success in business. And that has also led to success in life.

Remember, there is always a way. As long as you are persistent in taking extreme ownership of your life, then you are ready to be a leader. Leaders do not rely on other people to make decisions in their own life. They rely on the gifts and talents God has given them. If they have a shortfall in abilities, they then find a way to learn.

If you are ready to be that leader, it is time to get going in the right direction. There is no time like the present. You are only assured this very second. Carpe NOW! Be someone who is a leader and not a follower of the masses. Choose a disciplined life that is not about feeling good all the time. Feelings come and go, but your discipline needs to be here to stay. Do not allow your discipline to be like your feelings. Do not wait for the big aha moment. Time is precious, and your time is now. Use your intellect to take the first step.

Once you tell your mind to take that first step, your body will follow. You are the master of your own body. You are not enslaved to yourself. You tell yourself what to do when you want to do it. You want to accomplish a goal or dream. Well, get that mind working and tell that body to move. Once your body is in motion, your feelings will catch up. Your passion will be ignited. Though you do not need passion and feelings to accomplish your goals, those will come in due time. If you wait for the right feeling, you might wait your entire life.

This habit's challenge for you is to follow through with your commitments by taking ownership of your life and be the leader God designed you to be. Your chances are fleeting. Your life is a simple vapor. Reap the opportunity you have in front of you to take hold of your life. You are in the driver's seat. No longer be a passenger in your life. Put it in first gear and be the driver. Choose the hard way, not the easy way. If it is too easy and breezy, then it is not worth your time. Be the person who decides whether or not you are looking for the comfortable path or the hard one. The right path is the hard path. Choose your destiny today. The time is now. Choose to take The Great Trade. Carpe NOW, be disciplined, and reap the rewards.

Mindset

Someone who chooses to think positive
with a never-give-up mentality

> Whatever you constantly think about
> and focus upon, you move toward.
>
> —*Tony Robbins*

What mindset do you have?

The common misconception is that once you decide to change your life and head in a new direction, life will all be rainbows and butterflies. This is the furthest from the truth. After my life changed on July 15, 2001, and I decided to commit my life to a better, new way, life did not all of a sudden get hunky-dory. The truth is that once you decide enough is enough and make a commitment to move in a different direction, the real work starts. It makes sense to assume at that point, the hard work is in the past. It took work and effort to reach that decision, right? Correct. It did, but you now have to live up to the commitment. That is the hardest part: deciding that you are now a winner, and there is nothing standing in your way besides your own choices.

As I declared earlier, in my first life, I had a weak foundation. It took so much effort for me to fight at the very end when I was literally losing my mind. My past mistakes finally caught up with me—the constant agony and torment of being mentally tortured daily. It was an experience that was constantly and persistently attempting to tear me down. But it was all happening in my mind. Trying to battle my mind was, bar none, the most difficult fight I have ever faced in my life.

I am aware that many more challenges lie ahead in life. I am sure circumstances will put me on my knees. I also know that I have achieved a winning mindset. I have not quit. I do not give up on myself so easily. Especially when I know that the God of the universe has my back. He is my anchor and everything. Without Him, I do not have the strength to perform or live at the level that I want to achieve in this life. All glory be to Jesus forever and always. He is the solid rock on which I plant my feet. Separate from Him, I can accomplish few successes in life, but with Him I am a conqueror. I am on a journey that is not my own. I discovered my foundation and I understand my mission. There is absolutely nothing in my way besides myself.

I am fully aware that life could be cut short. But I live each day to the fullest for my God, my family, and the people that surround me who, I believe, need a leader, a fighter, and a lover who has their back. I fight for and defend what I believe in. That truth runs deep into my soul. It is everything to me. It allows me to operate at the highest level. Now, I do not always perform at the highest level. I like to say I fail more than I succeed. Actually, that's an exaggeration. The thing that allows me to know I am a winner—I will never give up. *You cannot lose if you do not give up.* My mission is in front of me, and that is my driving force. I am a man on a mission.

As soon as my life changed, I knew things would never be the same again. In an instant I was a different person. God cleansed my mind, body, and spirit. I was reborn as a new person. Yet there was a caveat. Even though I experienced an incredible transformation that I will never forget, and though God took away my mental torture and anguish, I still struggled with a very small amount of fear. It was incredible what God did to deliver my mind from that pain. All the distortions—the hallucinations—I was seeing and experiencing instantly, in the snap of a finger, went away when I decided to commit to God. Still, many little battles popped up ahead.

I knew beyond a shadow of a doubt that God had saved me. I committed my life to Him; I knew I could count on Him. I was a changed man. I had a tremendously strong belief that God was in my corner and there was nothing standing in my way. Hadn't I already succeeded in the ultimate victory? My soul was saved for all eternity. My debt of wrongdoing was forgiven. God no longer saw my shame. Yet there still was a battle. Whether you see it or not, there is a battle between good and evil. In many instances this battle is apparent, but there are plenty of instances where it flies under the radar. As is by design from the evil one.

I believe that after God changed my life, the demonic forces were not so happy about that. They lost the ultimate battle for my soul. But they knew many more opportunities would come to try to quench my enthusiasm—squash my belief in my newfound direction. That is exactly what happened. Evil forces would put fearful thoughts in my mind. Too many times to count after my life was spared, that fear tempted me to indulge it. I had to rely on the Bible to guide me. Day and night, I spent learning what God had to say about everything. I grew in knowledge and wisdom tremendously fast. I emptied my heart for God and gave Him 100 percent of me. The only real assurance I had that my sanity was sealed and safe was my complete dependence on God. In my mind every thought, every feeling, and everything I did had to be Spirit led.

God says in His word, the Bible, when you accept Him as your personal Savior and realize that He is the God of the universe, He will give you a Helper. This Helper is the Holy Spirit. This Holy

Spirit is God. The Spirit is a part of the Trinity. Maybe you have heard of this or not. It is best understood in experience by those who have accepted Christ as their Savior. The Trinity is the nature of God as the Father, the Son, and the Holy Spirit, all in One. The One true God. I understand it is hard to fathom, as we humans are limited by our understanding, comprehension, and knowledge. God's infinite wisdom and knowledge is far superior. He knows things that we cannot fathom, and if we could, it would probably melt our fragile brains. We would be in utter shock and disbelief if we knew all truth.

As in the case of many other things of the Bible, God wants us to step out in faith. However, there is a lot of scientific proof for God's existence. There is a very large portion of the books of the Bible, if you truly put in the time, in which there are plenty of factual answers available. There is also an element of faith; God wants us to trust Him. In my mind, it makes sense. If this is truly the most impactful decision someone will ever make, then we will probably not have every question answered. There is going to be an element of faith that we must trust in the living God, the all-present God, the all-knowing. Makes sense to me. God wants us to abandon some of our own reason to trust in Him. Now, this is not a completely blind faith, as some assert. As I just stated, the Bible has a lot of content that can be proven. Many of the items that cannot be proven are yet hard to disprove.

Unfortunately, I have seen many express harsh opinions about the Christian faith, trusting their own logical reasoning power over learning something that is not within their understanding or comfort zone. I am merely giving you my beliefs and opinions. If I am upsetting you, just know that is not where my heart is. Going back to the concept of this book, I am living up to who I authentically am. Someone who wears his heart on his sleeve. Someone who exposes all of who he is in the hopes of helping those who want help. My heart is not my own. God has restored me and given me a new heart. One that beats for people and not merely myself.

When I decided to put my faith in Jesus, I still had to fight many battles in my mind. It took many years for me to grow strong enough in my faith. To understand in time that my sanity is secure in Christ.

What God did on that beautiful day was deliver my sanity back to me. I did not deserve it. I absolutely did not earn it. I'd lived a self-centered and self-serving life. God took the worst, not the best, of people in choosing me. I knew I was not good enough; that is why He chose me. I did not deserve His blessings. I am miserably alone and unworthy without God. Given the opportunity to grow through my mental battles is something I am so abundantly blessed to have experienced. There is an unquenchable passion that lives in my soul.

Within the first couple of years after I devoted my life to God, certain circumstances would trigger past thoughts. These circumstances were my battlefield. For example, finding myself around people doing something that would not be pleasing to God, or being talked to by someone from the past I did not see often—who acted like I was still the same person, not realizing I was absolutely brand-new, who yet tried to pull me back into my old lifestyle. These sorts of situations would trigger emotions in me, bring fears to the surface.

I would ask myself questions like, *Maybe I did not change at all. Did I? Maybe it was all an illusion, leading up to the grand finale of my real fate. Is God even real? And if He is real, does He even care about me? Did he really save my sanity, or was that just by chance?* Countless questions then invaded my mind. I firmly believed these questions were not always my own thoughts. I believe it was evil forces trying to persuade me into the direction that was apart from God. Plenty of times, I literally had a panic attack from these fears. I would get down on my knees, praying to God to rescue and deliver me from these thoughts. At times God would instantly rescue me in that moment, but other times He would not. And those thoughts would linger.

Even in the worst moments, I knew what I was up against. It was a spiritual battle. Not for my soul, because that fate was already sealed with God, but a battle for my day-to-day lifestyle. A battle for the life I chose to commit to. I knew there are those who defy God's way and do not want to see God win in any capacity. They want to see evil triumph, even though they know their true fate. It was so bad at times that I would not only be on my knees, but I would open the word of God and start reading aloud scripture that was relevant and impactful. In these times I would sense the presence of demons around me, taunting my mind, trying to lure me away from God's truth. As I was reading the Word aloud on my knees, I sweated profusely, my heart pounding out of my chest. But even then, I knew I was going to get through these attacks. I had to withstand the battle that was right in front of me. That battle was for my mind. What epic battles they were.

These battles came at a moment's notice, when the enemy knew the opportunity was ripe. By enemy, I mean Satan and his demonic forces. These demonic forces would mentally attack me. If it happened, it would occur in the night in a quiet place. When I was around people and had distractions, these attacks were not prevalent. The enemy is smart. I knew God had my back. I knew I was already the victor, but God allowed me to endure these situations to grow in my faith. If it was not for these challenging times, I would not be half the man that I am.

From my radical transformation onward, God gave me the ability to sense the presence of evil in an area, room, or even people. Correspondingly, I could also sense God's presence. Fact: I had an extremely strong connection with God's spirit and the spirit world in general. To a lot of people, this is scary stuff. I get it. I did not enjoy the rough session of growth myself. I knew it was a reality, but I would rather not be the one experiencing it. But again, God had His reason for allowing it to happen.

There was an instance, back when I was in college at Joshua. Now, this was 2002, only a little over a year after I changed my life around. It was a late night. Just having gotten off work in town, I was walking back to the college. Joshua was located on top of a part of the mountain that was on the edge of the town near the woods. Students did not have access to cars, so we walked everywhere. The walk from the town back to college was roughly a mile—up a fairly steep grade—and at night it is pitch black. If you did not know where you were going, you could easily get lost. Mind you, nature was all around us—from bears, wolves, coyotes, mountain lions, bobcats, to Bigfoot, and we even had a Chupacabra—just kidding on the last two.

While walking back to camp, I sensed multiple demonic presences. I felt a battle looming. *Again, these battles were in my mind,* not physically in front of me. Sometimes battles in the mind are the hardest to deal with; in this case, get rid of. As I was headed towards my dorm room on campus, it was so dark I could hardly see my feet in front of me. Typically, we were told to always walk back in groups with a flashlight. Well, I got off work late and I had neither. I sucked it up, put on my big boy pants, and headed to campus. All the way up, I sensed these demonic forces. About halfway up the mountain, I started having dagger-like thoughts come through my head that I knew were not my own.

Thoughts like: *You are not mentally strong enough to bear these burdens. All the things you have seen were just a precursor to what you were about to experience in your ultimate doom. We are coming for you. You cannot win over us. You are not strong enough. You are going to lose your mind; give up on yourself. You are unworthy to be called a child of God. God is not going to protect you. Just wait: when you least expect it, we are coming for you and you will lose.*

As I was battling this spiritual attack, I made it back to my dorm room. To give you some understanding, when you are having a spiritual attack in your mind and you are aware of it, no one knows besides those in the battle. There is evil and there is good, and you are sandwiched right in the middle. Basically, no one could tell I was going through these battles. They were fights not just for my life but against all the wars for my mind. The temptation for me in these times was to believe that these thoughts were my own and that I in fact was losing my mind. Which potentially could send me down a rabbit hole of darkness and despair. But I would not allow myself to take that path; I would stand up for the truth in my mind.

It is very clear in God's word that in order to defend against these battles, we need to wear the full armor of God. Our faith is our shield; our helmet is our firm knowledge of our salvation in Christ, and the word of God is our sword that is used to fight back. Ephesians 6:13 through 17 says, "Therefore, take up the full armor of God, so that you will be able to resist in the evil day, and having done everything, to stand firm. Stand firm, therefore, having girded your loins with truth, and put on the breastplate of righteousness, and having shod your feet with the preparation of the gospel of peace; in addition to all take up the shield of faith which will be able to extinguish all flaming arrows of the evil one. And take the helmet of salvation, and the sword of the spirit, which is the word of God."

Knowing these verses gave me great comfort. They were my defense against the evil one. When I made it back to the dorm at my college, I got on my knees, opened the word of God, and started reading scripture. I would demand, in the name of Jesus Christ, that these demonic forces be gone. Not one time do I recall saying this aloud, and not instantly experiencing an absolute sense of peace right after. I understand it sounds hokey. Believe me when I say that I am a real skeptic. But God took a skeptic and made him a believer. God has proven His faithfulness. God has displayed His goodness in my life in multiple situations like this. He is faithful to equip those who accept Him and utilize His armor. That armor allowed me to conquer these battles. These battles brought challenging circumstances that I am incredibly grateful for. Without these difficult experiences to test my faith and overall mindset, I would not be nearly as indomitably strong as I am today.

Though I am not a veteran—I never served in the military—I am a veteran of spiritual battles, as I have fought them countless times. I know that battlefield quite well. The book of Ephesians 6:12 says, "For our battle is not against flesh and blood, but against the rulers, against the powers, against the world forces of this darkness, against the spiritual forces of wickedness in the heavenly places."

Believe me, these battles are going on all around us. They are not just a matter of life and death; they are matters of eternity. We humans live for only a short while, but after life on Earth is over, eternity waits for everyone. This is why there is a spiritual battle going on in the first place. It is to prevent as many people as possible from going to be with God for eternity and to stop you from living out your fullest potential in this life.

Whether you believe me or not, that is irrelevant. I know what I experienced. I was the one who lived it. I was the one who made it through these dark and challenging times. I was the one thrown into battle, who came out a victor. It is irrelevant whether you believe me or not, because the overall, arching point is that *I would have not made it through these battles without a firm mindset.* I had to *maintain a positive attitude* in the face of these situations. I knew I was going to win in the end since I was never going to give up. To me, giving up is not an option. I do not have a plan B. There is only plan A, which is to never give up. I will fight until my last breath in this life.

You have heard it said, you cannot lose if you never give up. I said it earlier in this book. I believe it to be true. It is as simple as thinking positively towards life and all life's circumstances. *Understand that life's not out to get you.* Life is working for you. Your circumstances are not too great to overcome. You have been given this beautiful gift; it's life with the freedom of choice. You have the freedom to choose whatever you want to choose. That is a key point. Whether you believe anything that I've said or not, you will decide what you believe, and I believe that is as it should be.

In my mind, it is right for you to get the freedom to choose what you want to. Freedom of choice is a beautiful thing. Just remember, with every choice you make, there is an outcome. With poor choices, you will have poor outcomes. With good choices, you will have good outcomes. Sometimes these rules will flip, but whatever choice you make, you must live with the consequences. You only get one life, so make the most of its many choices.

Even if you live in a country (or in circumstances) where hard-to-resist (or seemingly impossible-to-resist) pressures are making you do things you do not want to, at the end of the day the choice is always yours. Whatever you choose might have life-altering consequences. As illustrated in my life, even under the most extreme mental torture, I chose to say no, not yes. The best decision of my life. Choose your answer and move in that direction. You are the master of your mind. You tell your mind what to think, say, and *to the extent humanly possible* do. Try as they might, *no one has influence over your mind other than yourself.*

I am blessed to have gone through all of these mental battles. Those mental battles taught me that there is nothing that I cannot accomplish. Yes, my number one is God, who is in my corner, and you know, that is everything to me. But I am the owner of my mind; I tell my mind what to think, what to do, and how to operate. I take extreme ownership of all my thoughts. If I do not like how my mind is thinking, I start thinking about something entirely different— putting together a mental blueprint of how I need to think *in order to accomplish what I want to.*

God has given us these beautiful minds that we each possess. Our minds can be used to destroy us if we allow it, or they can be used to let us accomplish whatever we set our mind on. No person ever existed who fully understood the mind. It is incredibly intricate. It is beautifully and wonderfully made. Thinking about the human mind alone should challenge us to think about the big questions in life: *Is there a God? Why was I even created?* It makes sense to ask these questions because the mind is so vast and perfectly put together. This could not be merely by chance. Your mind was created by something beyond us. Beyond our simple comprehension. I am OK, knowing that I do not know everything. I lean on the One who, I believe, is in charge.

This winner's mindset needs to invade your every thought. If you have tendencies to get down on yourself, it is time to say enough is enough. Stop tearing yourself down. Build yourself up by thinking correctly about who you really are. You are amazing. You are one of a kind. There is no one else on this planet just like you. There is no one that has ever existed who is like you. You have been created perfectly as you are. You are blessed and perfectly designed; you must believe you are. Do not allow outside forces to dictate how you think. Regardless of any current storm or life situation, step up to the plate and knock the ball out of the park. It is time for you to hit a grand slam. This grand slam is your winning mindset.

Tony Robbins says—in person at his events—"The happiest people do not have the best of everything, they just make the best of everything." He also said, "I don't care what it is you've achieved, and the reason is because life is not about achieving the goals, life is about who you become in pursuit of those goals." [2] Choose to make the best of everything. Even if every single person in your life tells you otherwise, see the glass half full, not half empty. Remember, when you choose to make this decision to live a better way, it begins in your mind. Start thinking better. Like my story, it might not be easy. When you decide to go in a new direction, don't expect life to be peachy keen all of a sudden. It is probably going to get harder before it gets easier. Get your mind around the foreseeable and unforeseeable challenges; be excited about the challenges that lie ahead. Look those challenges in the eye and go to war with them.

Mindset is the last authentic habit in my list for a reason. Hopefully, you have learned in this book how to start cultivating the authentic you. There are many practical tools in this book to start chiseling away at the true you. You must apply all of these authentic habits to your life one by one. The order in which you do this is not fixed. It depends on your season in life. However, I designed this book for you to start with the first authentic habit, Foundation, and move all the way through the finishing touches to in the end achieve your authentic Mindset. Each one of these habits functions as a tool in discovering your authentic self. Another way to look at it, your mindset is the icing on the cake or the cherry on top. It is the final step that leads you to the Promised Land.

If you have not mastered all of these authentic habits, now is the time. At the end of the day, your mindset should be your driving force—what carries you all the way through to the end. It is something you will have to work on daily.

To be a positive person is not by chance or DNA trait. We choose to be positive or not. Choosing to be a positive person is choosing to be a titan for your success in life. *Being positive is a form of intelligence.* Choose to be intelligent today. Think highly of yourself. Think highly of those around you. Think highly of your circumstances.

Most importantly, think highly of your future. Your future is happening now, *as you read.* It is one minute away, one day away, one year away, one decade away, and one century away from now. What do you want to be written in the history books about you? Not everyone has the same ambitions and dreams. That is something I find to be beautiful. It would be a drag to have the same ambitions and dreams as everyone else. We are all designed with different wants and needs. The point is that you discover yourself and you adopt the mindset to see those goals and dreams become real—bring them to life.

You might find it challenging to apply everything that you have learned in this book. I expect that. Not everything will be the best fit for you and your life. Understand, I am just a man on a mission, trying to do his best. But I am not going to say and do everything correctly. Take what you want from these authentic habits and apply them to yourself. Be diligent to maintain that you are as strong as you say you are. Acquire the mindset that knows you will accomplish anything you want to. *Anything.* Never give up on yourself. Make the choice to give up, and you will not get very far in life.

However, if you choose to put in the work, be diligent in applying these authentic habits, and never give up on yourself, you will undoubtedly go far. And always be a winner. Maintain a firm mindset to know that there are no obstacles so difficult that you cannot overcome them. Accomplish what you set out to. God has given you many gifts. Use them. Know that your victory is inevitable because you will never give up. Do not let anyone or anything tell you otherwise. Maintain a strong winner's mindset until the end. Be an unstoppable force that will never quit on yourself.

Carpe NOW

Time to seize your best life this very second.

> Only one who devotes himself to a
> cause with his whole strength and soul
> can be a true master. For this reason
> mastery demands all of a person.
>
> —*Albert Einstein*

You did it! You made it this far. Assuming you have read and fully digested all of these authentic habits in this book, you have accomplished something great. You might be exhausted yet extremely excited about the future. There is a ton to digest in this book. It takes someone with guts who is willing to apply these authentic habits to life. Even with all of the practical tools in this book, it is not a given that you are going to apply them. The ball is in your court. The choice is yours to choose the authentic you, going forward. The real question is, are you up for the task? You have learned what it takes to discover the authentic you, but have you decided to go through with it?

One of my struggles after my life changed was forgiving myself for all the wrong I had caused others, all the wrong I'd caused myself, and all the wrong others had caused me. Though I committed to a new, better way on that life-changing day in July 2001, as time went on, a piece of me felt guilty about my past. To be honest, it was not my major struggle, but I was aware of it. I knew it had to be dealt with. I beat myself up, feeling that maybe my debt was too great, that the wrong I'd done was too large to be atoned for.

Then there was the wrong I'd done myself by my perverse lifestyle. These were all choices I made. I was the reason for my circumstances. Maybe not all of them, but some of them. I lived the life of pleasure, doing just as I pleased. That left me in the end literally losing my mind and having no real purpose in life. If it was not for God and His saving grace, I would have just been another lost soul. I am incredibly grateful that God rescued me from myself, as I was the one who was at fault. I chose a life of pride and selfishness. Obviously, life on my terms was not working.

Of course, there was the harm that was being caused to me. I believe the majority of it was unintentional, but it was causing me pain, built up over time. My reaction had been to act out in a way that left my life going down a spiral of doom. There were a lot of inconsistencies in my upbringing that were not my fault and not necessarily my parents' either. Unfortunately, I was severely affected by my parents' divorce.

After I gave my life to God, I knew my debt was forgiven by God on paper. But the feelings I had were not all gone. Some were still very much alive. I knew without a shadow of a doubt that after I acknowledged what Jesus Christ did for me on the cross and I committed my life to Him, I was eternally forgiven. However, God allowed some of that burden to remain, I believe, for me to learn from it. I had to learn how to forgive.

Learning to forgive others is not easy for most people. It does not come naturally. It is a burden that is anchored in our human souls. Even those who know God has forgiven their own debt struggle to forgive themselves. It is especially difficult for them to forgive themselves. Forgiveness in general is one of the greatest struggles we humans face. We feel shame, grief. We've caused pain to those we love. It's hard to let that go. But in order for any to discover their authentic self and seize their new life, their best life, forgiveness must be a part of the process.

There are people in your life who have caused you pain. This pain could be physical or emotional. Whether on purpose or unintentional, it still caused you a tremendous amount of anguish. Maybe that pain is something you have chosen to live with on a daily basis. That pain burdens you from progressing forward. Maybe you have tried to get rid of it but no luck. You might even believe you are stuck with it. I do not fully understand your situation, as it is unique to you. My recommendation is, if possible, to find this person and meet them where they are at.

If possible, have a discussion with them. Communicate to them the pain that they caused you. Lay 100 percent of it on the floor. Let them know every little detail. All of your feelings and all of your thoughts, expose to them. If you are not able to have a discussion with this person, maybe you can simply speak *at* them without a response. If this person is no longer alive or is not accessible, then you are going to have to pretend to have this discussion with them. But you fundamentally have to do it. Find a quiet place. Do it by yourself in front of a mirror or speak aloud to them, as though they were in the room. It sounds silly, but there is power in being able to elaborate your thoughts and feelings out into the world.

After you have said every possible little thing about the harm that was done to you and the way it made you feel, then and only then, you must forgive them. It does not make what they did OK. It does not say what they did was justified. But it releases the burden from you and places it on them. They then will have a choice to make the next move or not; their response is irrelevant. By holding on to that pain, you are only damaging your future progress. Most likely, the individual who wronged you has moved on, but for whatever reason, you cannot. You have not been able to move on because you have not exposed your deepest, darkest feelings to that person.

Once you have declared everything you can possibly tell this person, forgive them and move on. In the most sincere and genuine ways possible, look them dead in the eyes straight through to their soul. Let them know you have forgiven them, and you are moving on with your life. Again, this person might not even be physically in front of you—might not even be alive or accessible. But you still must have this conversation. Remember, this conversation is primarily for you. To let them know that you will no longer be bogged down by past trauma.

Tell them you are a new person, going forward. You have discovered the authentic you. You will no longer be bound by the past but are only living in the present. You are living in this very moment, ready to seize every opportunity that is in front of you. Life is no longer working against you; it is working for you. Life is working to assist you. To help you accomplish all of your dreams and ambitions. Once you have forgiven this person, the weight you carry will be immediately lifted off you. You will feel as if you are floating on clouds. Your burdens will be light, your temperament will be shifted, and your life will never be the same.

It is one thing to forgive someone else, but it is another level of difficulty, I have found, to forgive yourself. We are our own worst enemies. We are our worst critics. We get down on ourselves for the things we have done to others and ourselves. For most of us, it is not easy to forgive ourselves, as most of us do not feel worthy to be forgiven. There is a level of pain that we keep as fuel to remind us of where we have been and what we have done. I am here to tell you that it is not fuel but a fire that consumes your very purpose and drive. If you want to be unleashed and achieve a level of fulfillment that you have never before experienced, you have to let the past go.

If you are harboring mistakes or traumas, it is time to let them go. Have a discussion with yourself. Find a quiet place where you can hear and write down your thoughts. Bring a journal. Make sure you have that journal by your side. Journaling is a weapon to be used to understand yourself. Do not take that weapon for granted.

Write out all of the pains you caused or experienced. All of the things that you do not forgive yourself for. All of the past pains that fester in your mind. Once you have completely written everything down, it is time to understand that pain on a deeper level. Think about each incident as if it were yesterday. Remember what it was like to be where you were at that moment. Remember what it was like to do exactly what you did to cause harm to others or yourself. Or whatever traumatic experience you had to endure.

Whether you caused the pain or someone else did, look at that person and let them know you forgive yourself. You are no longer going to be shackled by past mistakes. No longer going to just move in a direction aimlessly, but instead, from now on, to move in a direction full of purpose and passion. You do not have the mental energy anymore to waste time on this past incident. You are deciding right now to move on with your life. All of this must be vocalized clearly and precisely. Do not leave out a thought or word. Be intentional with each and every word you speak.

If you wronged someone else, in some cases it might be beneficial to meet with that person. Again, meet face to face, eye to eye, and verbally repeat every transgression you did that wronged that person. Maybe to the other person, it's long forgotten, not something they even care about. It might not have even affected them. That really does not matter. This is all about forgiving yourself. You are looking to release yourself from those burdens. To acknowledge those feelings, to understand them, to forgive yourself and finally move on from the past.

When you reach that place of true forgiveness, there are not many feelings like it—the feeling of knowing that you are finally free. You have wiped your debt free and clear in your mind. That will be an amazing feeling. One that will take some effort on your part, but it will be worth it. It will put you in a position to move forward with excellence in every area of your life. You will have a hard time applying these authentic habits if you do not think you are worth the effort. If you do not seek forgiveness and start fresh, you will always find yourself going back to square one over and over. Do not let that be you. Decide that you are going to move your life forward to a new level of authenticity.

Maybe you have never believed in God. Maybe you believe in God, but you do not have a relationship with Him. Possibly after reading this book and listening to my life experiences, you realize there is a God and want to know Him. If that is the case, there is a place for you in God's loving arms. God desires deeply to have a one-on-one relationship with you. There is nothing you can do to earn His favor. His love and forgiveness are for everyone. He gives that to you freely in the person of Jesus Christ.

Jesus not only existed two thousand years ago, but He also proclaimed Himself to be God. Through many eyewitnesses and verifiable written testimonies, He performed many miracles and incredible signs. He performed no greater miracle than predicting His exact death on a cross by crucifixion. The story goes, God came to save His people, the Jews, but His people did not recognize Him. Jesus proclaimed Himself to be God, and the Jews did not believe He was the Messiah, the chosen One, God. For that reason, they had the Romans put Jesus to death.

Jesus not only foresaw exactly how He would die but also all the little details that led up to His crucifixion. Before His death He also proclaimed that He would not be bound by the grave but that He would rise from the grave three days later. There were thousands of eyewitnesses, and there is verifiable written testimony that He did in fact rise from the grave. Just as surely as Christopher Columbus sailed the open seas to discover new land and Michelangelo created a masterpiece at the Sistine Chapel, Jesus did in fact rise from the grave. Arguably, this is a verifiable fact. There is more proof than people realize and acknowledge. There is more evidence that He rose from the grave than that He did not.

That piece of information is pivotal. If Jesus did in fact rise from the grave, then you would have to take into account everything that He stated in His short life as from God because that is who He declared Himself to be. Facts: Jesus was a man who existed for only thirty-three years. He is indisputably the single most influential person in history. Crazily enough, though Jesus died at thirty-three, He only began His ministry at thirty years of age. He did not start proclaiming who He was or performing any miracles until the age of thirty. Jesus changed the world forever in a short three years. Better yet, Jesus changed the world in just a few moments on the cross when He bore all humanity's sins on His back.

Josh McDowell and Sean McDowell, co-authors of the best-selling book *More Than a Carpenter*, with over fifteen million copies sold, said it precisely best: Jesus was either "a liar, a lunatic, or Lord and God."[3] Which was it? Draw your own conclusion. When you truly review the evidence, it is staggering—actually mind-blowing. But you know as well as I do, people typically do not do the necessary due diligence to find out for themselves. Typically, if people do not understand something, they either ignore it or bash it. My challenge for people who struggle with the merits of what I am presenting: go find out the truth for yourself. I guarantee if you knock on that door, you will get an answer, whether you like it or not.

Jesus not only was God, but He is the living and active God. He is everywhere all the time. He is all knowing and all-capable. There is nothing outside of His scope or reach. He knows you by name. He knows you so intimately that He even knows the hair count on your head. If you believe as I do that Jesus Christ is God and that He did in fact sacrifice Himself for our sins, simply have a conversation with Him. Let Him know that you believe in your heart and with your whole being that He is the living God. Trust Him with your life. Live as He would want you to live a life for Him and others. Jesus will take care of you. I know this to be true. He has taken care of me for twenty-two years. He also has changed billions of lives over generations. He is not stopping anytime soon.

If you have no interest in believing in God or having a relationship with Him, I am not here to pressure you otherwise. As I have declared I am giving you my everything by sharing my complete authentic heart with you. I only want to see you live your best life. I believe that the best life is in Jesus. I believe that He is the true firm foundation of everyone's life. If you are not there, I hope one day you will reconsider, but as for now, just know that I love you and want the best for you.

Hopefully, you are now at a place where you have completely embraced forgiveness. You have decided to forgive those around you, and most importantly yourself. Now you are ready to start fresh. You are ready to live your most authentic self. You might have a feeling of jubilation pumping through your body, leaving you feeling full of life. When you allow those burdens to go and you've decided to be fully empowered by the new you, there is nothing stopping you. Even though you are at this place of excitement and freshness, there is still work to be done.

Now you must make sure to be a master at each of the ten authentic habits. Your mastery of each is going to be the difference between you succeeding by reaching your full potential or not. By now I hope that you understand what it takes to find your true Foundation. To clarify your personal Mission in life. You can now create a Blueprint for success that maps out your journey. You are fully aware that it is going to take Perseverance to push past the difficult times. That your personal Fitness needs to be one of your top priorities. You are committing to finding a Community of people to support you. You realize that your life is not just about you but about exhibiting Selflessness towards others—serving people with your whole heart. That being a lifelong student is all a part of the Growth process. You understand that your Discipline will be tested, yet you will remain positive and be consistent. Finally, you know that it takes a strong Mindset to steer the ship of your life. To achieve this level of personal success and fulfillment in life, you must always remember to remain diligent in all ten authentic habits.

If you have truly applied all of these ten authentic habits, then you are on your way to living your best life. There is nothing holding you back. It has been my privilege and honor to lead you down this path of finding your authentic self. My heart so desires to see you win and succeed in life. I know that if you put in the work, apply these authentic habits, and never give up, you will be successful in your journey. There is nothing or no one that can stop you now. You are a force to be reckoned with. You are unstoppable, if you believe you are.

Remember, it is YOU versus YOU. The only person who can get in your way is yourself. Take extreme ownership of your life and live your best life. The time for action is this very second. Your time is NOW. You are alive; that means you have unfinished business. You have a purpose that will feed your passion. That passion will carry you to your destination. You will encounter roadblocks, but they will not stop you. Nothing will stop you. You are relentlessly in pursuit of a full, purpose-filled, rich, life. A life that is led by your most authentic self. Your authentic self is thankful to be found, as now the shackles are off, your burdens are finally lifted, your life has a reason, and things will never be the same. There is only one thing left to do, Carpe NOW!

ACKNOWLEDGMENTS

Long after I am gone, I want my children, Tenley Grace and Kingston James Barrena, to know that I am proud of you. I know with every fiber in my body and soul that the both of you will grow up to build a rich legacy of your own. You will change the world for the better of all. My love for you is the truest love I possess. It has no limits or bounds. Daddy would do anything for you. I only ask that you be who God created you to be . . . the authentic you. Both uniquely and distinctly different from each other, you are amazing. Daddy desires for you to live your best life. An abundant, blessed life. That life is designed to be in relationship with God, as He is the reason for everything. Trust in Him, as He will never let you down. Daddy loves you so much.

Next, my beautiful bride, Ashlee Britt Barrena. Cliché yet true: you complete me, my love. There is no person I wish to live and thrive besides than you. You are "Ashlee, My Love" which, is for always and forever.

Mom, you believed in me when many did not. Thank you for being the best mom a son could have. I love you, Mom. You are my person and the reason I am alive. Dad, we have a lot of history together. Some good and some challenging. I know you did your best. I love you for that. You taught me a lot. You did good, Dad. I admire you for who you have become, a good man. I love you, Dad.

To my brothers, Jeffrey and Dylan. You are both so close to me despite our differences. I am always in your corner—as I know you are always in my corner. I love you both tremendously.

To all those others who have been a part of my journey in some way or another. Without the connections I've made over the years with you, this book would not be possible. I have learned and grown from our relationships. You know who you are . . .

Thanks for reading my book. I hope it has changed your life the way it has changed mine.

Connect with me at

JakeBarrena.com

ABOUT THE AUTHOR

Jake Barrena is a man on a mission passionate about living his best life and helping others do the same.

As an entrepreneur, he has started over twelve businesses, learning from both successes and failures. He currently owns a successful real estate company in Orange County, California.

He loves staying in top physical shape and has become skilled in many extreme sports. Spending time with his wife and two kids is among his top priorities.

Most importantly, he is a man of devout faith, who lives his values. He loves to create and build ways to impact people for good.

He firmly believes to live a best life one must master authenticity, which is God's original design.

Notes

1   Simainc, "The Science of Stress," Stress Tips and Tricks | Healthy Living | SLMA.
2   Catherine Clifford, "Tony Robbins: This Is the Secret to Happiness in One Word," Tony Robbins: This is the secret to happiness in one word (cnbc.com).
3   Josh D. McDowell and Sean McDowell, excerpt from the updated inspirational classic *More Than a Carpenter*, online at Jesus: Liar, Lunatic or Lord? - The Arc (tyndale.com). Based on a C. S. Lewis quote in *Mere Christianity*.

Made in the USA
Las Vegas, NV
21 September 2024

95548557R00115